My Father took me to the Circus

My Father took me to the Circus

PRUE WILSON

Darton Longman and Todd
London

First published in 1984 by
Darton, Longman and Todd Ltd
89 Lillie Road, London SW6 1UD

ISBN 0 232 51615 4

British Library Cataloguing in Publication Data

Wilson, Prue
My father took me to the circus.
1. Monastic and religious life of women
I. Title
248.8'943   BX4210

ISBN 0–232–51615–4

Phototypeset by Input Typesetting Ltd London SW19 8DR
Printed in Great Britain by Anchor Brendon Ltd
both of Tiptree, Essex

To Mary
Mother of Jesus
the Woman who believed the impossible
and whose song is
the Magnificat

Contents

Acknowledgements

My great gratitude goes to those who have made this book possible; to all my sisters of the Society of the Sacred Heart on earth and in heaven, especially those of England and Malta; to my family and friends who may recognize, as their own, ideas I claim to be mine; to the late Joan Gummer who asked for and published an article in *The Ship*, the magazine of St Anne's College, Oxford; to Alanna Hornby who showed it to Lesley Riddle of Darton, Longman and Todd; to Lesley's encouragement to turn it into a book; to my provincials in England and Uganda, Sisters Elizabeth Smith and Doreen Boland, for giving me time to write it; to Dr Mary Hallaway for continuing the good work of many years by challenging my assumptions and making me acknowledge my limitations; to my patient community in this place of prayer in the Brecon Beacons for listening, commenting and reviving my drooping spirits; above all, to Sister Margaret Tindal for typing and retyping illegible drafts, and to Sister April O'Leary for keeping my hand to the plough, for finding lost pages, and for creating a semblance of order around me; to Laurella Matthews, my one-time Oxford tutorial partner, for agreeing to join forces with April as critic, corrector of spelling, syntax, punctuation, and for seeing the proofs through to publication; to Jan Spiller and Sisters Madeleine Simon, Margaret Bunbury and Patritia Hayes for a marathon of typing, correcting and duplicating.

I am grateful to Victor Gollancz Ltd for permission to quote from *Bourgeois Land* by Iain Crichton-Smith, and to Dr Elizabeth Templeton for allowing me to quote her personal comments on the poem; and also to Magdalen Goffin for permission to quote from the work of her father, E. I. Watkin.

PRUE WILSON
Llanerchwen, Brecon
1 September 1983 – 31 January 1984

Prologue

The title of this book originates in a memory of long ago. I was three or four and my father's regiment was stationed in the Isle of Wight. My Roman Catholic mother was away, and my father and our old nurse, Ann Howard, rashly decided to take me to some particularly splendid Sunday service. It was held in a vast tent, and there was the regimental band to accompany the several hundred highland voices as they roared the hymns. I hated it, and wept loud and long because of the noise which seemed deafening and unbearable. I think I must have been made to stick it out as I have a memory of prolonged misery and the picture in Ann's prayer book of the woman sweeping around for her lost groat, which was obviously used to distract me.

A few days later my father took me to a circus. There was panic at the sight of another vast tent, and the dreadful distant sound of a band. I yelled and kicked saying that I did not want to go to church. Then a sense of complete trust swept over me as he picked me up in his arms and said that it was all right. It was not church, but a circus and I would like it. The ecstasy that followed remains profoundly of God, who was and is my Father, and of a circus. He is always the one who carries me to a joy I never knew existed.

So the image of the circus is important to me. It is archetypal and flamboyant; behind it is the remembrance of childhood, and in it every human person has a star part. If I were to imitate Plato and invent my own version of his allegory of the cave, it would be the allegory of the circus; but instead I shall imitate Jesus and say, 'The kingdom of heaven is like this: it is a great gathering of people, each one a performer and each one rejoicing in the performance. It is a show on the road, and its stage is a circle of light in which each discovers what it means to be uniquely, miraculously gifted.

The night sky vision of the universe is its big top. What parts will be taken up by whom will never be written on the programme, but the whole of the living world will be caught into the joy and magic and skill of the performance, and every act will show us something more about freedom and interdependence and trust.'

Henri Nouwen[1] sees men and women religious as the clowns in this circus of life, and that fits my parable perfectly. May we find our place in the kingdom as those who are 'always knocked down but never knocked out'.[2] May we be the nonsense people who, wherever we are and whatever we do, bring laughter with us, and the reassurance that to be fallible and very foolish is to be human, and that to be human is the only way for us to be the glory of God.

---

[1]   Henri J. M. Nouwen, *Clowning in Rome*, trans. J. B. Phillips, Image Book 1979.
[2]   2 Corinthians 4:8.

1. Good News

'Nuns is noos,' said a genuine, green-eye-shaded newsman holding up an English nun friend of mine with levelled microphone. This was on a U.S.A. university campus during the Vatican II hurricane of change that swept the Roman Catholic world of the 1960s.

The news he referred to was the shock of a shattered image, headlines for a Roman Catholic press still catering for a public content to accept that the world was conveniently divided into men, women and nuns. The fact that these headlines told horror stories of nuns showing their hair, shortening their skirts, or discarding their veils was the trivialization of some of the implications of the Vatican Council's call to a renewal of religious life. It was a call to all religious, but the congregations and orders of men did not provide fodder for popular Roman Catholic funny stories, cartoons or gossip columns. The orders and congregations of women did, because the central unacknowledged change for them was that the call to renewal included a recognition by the Church that they were not only religious, but women.

All this was more than twenty years ago. I have been a nun, or rather, to use the correct term, a religious sister, for forty years. I am aware therefore that for half my religious life I experienced the triumphalist, outwardly rock-like immobility of the pre-Vatican-II Church, and loved it. I lived through the irruption into Vatican II of the unseen inward turmoil of the Church and by it was shaken out of my complacency. Finally, I am still here, observing with misgiving the conservatism which is again taking us over both inside and outside the Church. The history of the second half of my religious life moves from the visionary 1960s through the disillusioned 1970s into the conservative 1980s in a sequence like a speeded-up film. There is already a library full of scholarly and critical books reviewing this period from the sociological points of view: at world level, emergent-country level, women's movement level, Roman Catholic ecclesiastical level. God knows how many more books are still to come. Perhaps therefore it is not just presumption but a sure sign of dotage that from within the Roman Catholic scene I should add yet another volume to the list. But forty years is a good biblical space of time and for me, as a religious, it has been co-existential with a revolutionary period in the salvation history of the people of God. My personal salvation history may reflect something of this. So I want to write about my experience of evolution and revolution within myself and in the congregation to which I belong. It is a narrow experience, but it is mine. Mine too is my faith in a future for religious life and my conviction that it will have new shape and be prophetic for the whole Church.

Resistance to new shape is inevitable. Jesus, whose friends stored their wine in leather bottles, talked about new wine in old skins. Alas for us Roman Catholics: the new wine of the Spirit has been and will continue to be spilt unless we prepare new skins to contain it, and do not merely patch the old. We must also persuade those for whom the old wine was delicious to believe at least in the potential goodness of the new.

It is not part of my self-imposed brief to concentrate on the women's liberation aspect of my assessment of the present scene and of my vision of the future. But, like the cheerfulness of Dr Johnson's young friend, it is an aspect which will no doubt keep breaking in. Of course the convergence in the 1960s of the insights of the women's movements with those of women religious was an important part of our growing self-awareness, especially in the U.S.A., where women religious represent a larger body of a more politically influential Church than in England. Religious in the U.S.A. were also more closely in touch with, and involved in, the life of a large number of university and college campuses at a time of interior student unrest, civil rights demonstrations, and burnt army draft cards. In fact they were exposed to the questioning of authority and of accepted patterns in a way denied to many of their sisters in other parts of the world. Women religious in other countries were stirring of course, and the Churches of Holland and Latin America were opening up new dimensions of incarnational and liberation theology which would force us all to re-examine some of our assumptions.

Meanwhile the invasion of the West by Eastern mysticism, and of the East by Western seekers, heightened our awareness of prayer as a way of life. This was valuable at a time when a sense of the transcendent seemed to be diminishing. But women religious of the U.S.A. should be thanked by their sisters everywhere for their readiness to explore new frontiers, to communicate what they had found beyond them, and to face the inevitable censure this entailed.

Of course there was disarray among the members of the various congregations and orders of women religious. Each individual nun of the time under sixty or even under seventy belonged in her upbringing to the twentieth century, even if it were a twentieth century with marked cultural differences. Since the day of her entry into the noviciate she had been asked to adopt a manner of life and dress of the mid-nineteenth century, to put it at the latest. Some of the older orders kept a manner of life that belonged to far earlier periods of history, and some congregations of great apostolic vision, founded in the twentieth century itself, adopted monastic customs. But – men, women, nuns? It would surprise me to know if any nun in any country from within the museum that had been built around her, had ever thought of herself as other than woman. It was the world that we kept outside that neutered us, even if it was our fault that it did so. As a woman, therefore, as well as a nun, each religious found herself swept away from the historic past into the twentieth century she thought she had given up and she was allowed a very short time to readapt. In view of the speed of the transition there was an inevitable sense of lost identity, lost balance and direction, and a cataclysmic fall-out of membership from the orders and congregations. There was also, for many of those who held on, relief: hope, fresh air, and a rediscovery of the essential in religious life. But for the lay men and women who had neutered the nun, shock, disillusionment and hurt predominated. Landmarks and certainties were disappearing in what seemed to be not just a hurricane of change but a whirlwind of destruction. Nuns were an important symbol, and that nuns should change so suddenly from a loved and well established way of life added to the bewilderment. For the average Roman Catholic of the time, nuns were news all right. Bad news.

Looking back and realizing that I was one of the disappearing landmarks, a living symbol of the unchanging that has changed, makes me see how short we are of meaningful symbols in the Church today. The Roman Catholic conservative movements declare a sense of their loss just as much as they declare a fear of change. Change is necessary, but liturgical impoverishment, deprivation of mystery and beauty, lead to a hunger that has a right to the food for which it craves. But beauty is the inexplicable shining forth of something true to its inner self. In the Christian context symbol must be a sign of the truth, not of magic or illusion. Nuns are a visible sign of the mystery of a primal relationship with God, just as marriage is a visible sign of the self-transcendence of human loving. The living out of both the marriage commitment and the commitment of the religious are a sign of the love that is God. But the outward manner of declaring this through marriage, its conventions and customs, changes to meet the needs of the age to which it belongs, unself-consciously creating its own liturgy of life. The way of commitment in religious community, on the other hand, can be statically ritualized and thus the sign becomes remote from the mystery it signifies. But the mystery-hungry people of God are loath to lose their proudly guarded living symbols. They believe that to hold on to them keeps the mystery enshrined, but before long the mystery has become magic, and its safe-guarding a form of idolatry.

I experienced something of this in the early transitional years after the Vatican Council. Looking at myself and at my sisters I could understand the pain at the loss of symbol, but found myself saying: 'Poor old nuns'. For, disproportionately admired, disproportionately despised, well wrapped up in fancy dress, pedestalled and neutered, what an immeasurably valuable symbol we provided: for some we were magic prayer-power, for others a sign of sexual masochism, horrifying in its pornographic projection. But for those who loved us, the retention of as much of the monastic structures as possible still recalled to faith in the glorious 'folly' of the cross. For those who had ears to hear and eyes to see we pointed to a way of life that looked steadfastly heavenward even as we spent ourselves in availability for, and service of, our neighbour. We pointed to a way of life which died daily with the still crucified Christ. For those who had ears to hear and eyes to see it was all satisfyingly recognizable. How incomprehensible that change from it should be asked for by the hierarchical Church.

The change was asked for because of the new insights of theology. Religious responding to the call to renewal realized only gradually that their way of life reflected a theology still locked in the great divide of sacred versus secular, Christian versus the world. It was a way of life often over-concentrated on a crucified Christ and on a theology of the cross. For all of us the new vision of the Church took time to become part of a new motivating power.

It was the Church's recognition of the need of a period for assimilation, that allowed freedom for a time of experimentation in living out community. This was an unprecedented opportunity for self-examination and growth in which existing constitutions were suspended, chapters involving the whole bodies of religious orders and congregations were called and a search for new relevance instigated. The opportunity opened by the Church to religious was the source of inspiration, although the Conciliar and post-Conciliar documents on religious life were disappointing.

However, with hindsight, this too could be called providential. Theology must grow out of life-experience. The Church could write about herself and her place in the world with Spirit-filled confidence because, beneath apparent immobility, Vatican II was separated from Vatican I by ninety years of dynamic subterranean self-questioning. There was little of this in the cloister. If the documents on religious life had therefore formulated a theology, they would have handed out a blue print and demanded conformity. As it was, they invited discernment and experiment, and a way was opened to religious during these years of experiment enabling them to reflect on what they did and why they did it. What was the mystery of the kingdom hidden in today's reality for which they must search, and how should their manner of life best reflect their purpose? During this time mistakes were made, but when sisters are news now, it is over matters that are serious.

The new conservatism finds this search dangerous, but we must be allowed to continue it so that our way of life can

create new patterns. As community we need to be a new
symbol of a fresh understanding of the radicality of the
Gospel.

If only the institutional Church which called us to renewal
could trust the motives behind our experimentation. It is hard
for a self-consciously visible Church to trust something so
invisible as motivation. Nonconformity to expected pattern is
always a threat to authoritarianism. But the Church will be
the poorer if it does not trust the faithful discernment of
so obedient, hardworking, dedicated, long-suffering prayer-
orientated a body of its faithful as its nuns and sisters. They
represent the largest organized group within it, the members
of which are prepared not only to stand up and be counted
but to offer themselves body and soul for its life-long service.

Meanwhile we have got to believe in ourselves, and
remember that nonconformity for the sake of the kingdom is
of the essence of Christian life, and therefore of religious life.
The founding fathers of the great religious orders challenged
the set patterns of their time and reminded their Christian
world what the Gospel was about. Benedict, Francis, Dominic
and Ignatius Loyola, to take the usual key figures, not only
experienced a charismatic call that transformed their lives,
but were able to communicate this experience. As others
responded, echoing in themselves a like call, the experience
had to be codified. But however the founder's experience was
codified, something put into words always tends to become,
in the hands of worthy men and women, the letter that kills.
In the hands of the less worthy it becomes something to be
largely ignored. The Church has always been invigorated by
the revolutionary rediscovery of the Gospel by the original
pattern-breakers and their immediate successors. But what in
them was revolutionary, a breaking through the boundaries
of their age, became in time a conservative pattern too rigidly
adhered to, or was shelved as an impossible dream too
exacting to be lived. So renewal, rebirth, new discovery of
new ways of pattern-breaking, must be continuous in a living
Church.

For those of us who responded to the Council's call to
seek renewal by a rediscovery of the initial inspiration of
our founders or foundresses, the challenge consisted in being
obliged to question what was revered. When we did so we

were often surprised to discover the founding vision much less structured than we had supposed.

This was particularly the case with women religious. Those who had adopted some modified form of the rule of the great founding fathers, had sometimes to question their own conformity to a pattern that seemed part of their identity but which had been shaped to match an outdated concept of women. Those like the Carmelites, Poor Clares, Second Order Dominicans or the Benedictines, who were living the primitive form of their rule, found themselves aware that it had been shaped for them in a world very different from our own. Those of us women religious who belong to different traditions discovered time and again that the prophetic vision of a foundress had been suppressed, distorted beyond recognition, or quietly channelled into cloistered controllability by the Church of the day. Angela Merici had a pre-Jesuit dream of apostolic religious life: it was changed and cloistered. Mary Ward's vision was strongly Jesuit, shaped by an England of the Elizabethan martyrs: it was simply not allowed to be. Vincent de Paul did his best to prevent his Daughters of Charity from becoming 'religious' in order that they could serve Christ in the poor with freedom, and even a saint like Francis de Sales could not save Jane Frances de Chantal and her nuns of the Visitation from being redirected into the strictest cloister. Of my own nineteenth-century congregation I shall write later. The point here is to recognize that pattern-breaking for the sake of the kingdom, expressive of the insights of contemporary theology and responding to the needs of the world, is for the first time open to us as women religious. The new shaping of a Gospel way of life is ours, but our search in the Spirit must show that we have vision and that our experimentation is for the sake of the kingdom, and not a way of escaping its demands.

And the men? I feel like St Paul on marriage that I have nothing to say but would wish them to be like ourselves.[1] The congregations of Brothers have a past, a present and a future very close to the apostolic congregations of women. Their clear declaration of religious vocation as other than the vocation to the priesthood is of immense relevance in the Church today. The older orders have become increasingly

[1] cf. 1 Corinthians 7.

priestly, a fact which perhaps needs examination. The priestly orders of necessity are enmeshed in two areas of self-scrutiny, as religious and as priests; and they must help us to see better what is the place of the priesthood in the Church of today and tomorrow. But whether we are men needing to question the inevitability of equating priesthood with a call to religious life, or women questioning why a strongly felt call to the priesthood should be denied them in or out of congregations or orders, let us all increasingly beware of sacrilized patterns or sacred symbols and be ready to be fearless nonconformists in the footsteps of our founders and foundresses.

The Church is necessarily caught up in the general muddle which is the reality of being human. And human beings are always trying to impose patterns on the confusion of life or to break the patterns others have made. Pattern-making is not only sociological; it is also the artist creatively at play or the historian reading a pattern into events.

Twenty years before Vatican II, in his book *Catholic Art and Culture*,[2] E. I. Watkin read such a pattern into the history of Christianity, looking back at what he saw to be the ages of Christendom since Classical Autumn, to Christian Spring, and through the Summer periods of the Middle Ages and the Renaissance, each manifesting its ethos through architecture, art and the emergence of a great religious order. He suggested that we of the twentieth century were on the brink of a new spring, an age of the Holy Spirit. Taking up some of his earlier thinking in an essay on 'The future of Roman Catholicism', written in the mid-nineteen sixties, he saw the Church of the future not only as part of this age of the Spirit but as a Church concerned less with being visible than with being contemplative, a Church in which 'the whole people of Yahweh were prophets'.[3]

Whether we choose to call our present time the age of the Holy Spirit or not, ours is certainly an age when the Spirit is mightily active. Will a new religious order be founded which will affect us all by the intensity of its charismatic relevance? Is it with us already in the Gospel simplicity of the Little Brothers and Sisters of Charles de Foucauld, or in the contem-

[2]   E. I. Watkin, *Catholic Art and Culture*. Burns and Oates 1942.
[3]   Numbers 11:29.

plative ecumenism of Taizé, showing a way of life which creates community across denominational barriers? Is it through Mother Theresa, a prophet in action of the charity that is the only valid sign of Christ's kingdom? There is pattern-breaking and remaking too in the secular institutes, for example the Focolari with their undenominational unstructured outreach.

In all these forms of community there is a common factor: men and women who respond together to a shared vision in different patterns of commitment. This is present also in the basic communities of Latin America which reflect something of the Christianity of the early Church and may become the model for the Church of tomorrow. If these ways of community and commitment are prophetic it may be that the outdated epithet 'religious' will disappear – the adjective, but not the way of life, voluntarily 'bound' in a primal commitment to Christ, and to the Community of those who find the bonding a sign of response to God's fidelity.

This need not mean the disappearance of existing orders and congregations. In the history of the Church the older patterns of religious life formed a springboard for the new, but could not remain unaffected by the new vision. Fidelity to the Gospel on the part of those already founded will, therefore, help to open the way to others for new forms of radical Christian commitment and they in their turn will modify us as they widen our understanding of the following of Jesus. Those of our congregations or orders less open to change and modification will die, whatever the good they have achieved in their time. No way of life can be at once dynamically Gospel and, at the same time, a reassurance to over-anxious respectability by refusing to change – least of all in the airport culture of today.

I find myself unnerved by the smug assurance of that paragraph. Airport culture with its connotation of smooth, impersonal, material efficiency may be a good enough description of the First World, but it is singularly inept as a description of our planet in the nineteen eighties – a bent world over which the Holy Ghost may brood but which seems bent to the shape of man the destroyer. In this age of the Holy Spirit, if we are right so to name it, two-thirds of the world's population starve, while one-third spends its excess resources not merely on planned self-destruction but on the destruction

of the other two-thirds as well. This fact is kept relentlessly
before our apparent powerlessness, mesmerizing most of us
into inaction. In such a world why speculate about the future
of what we at present describe as religious life? What can it
possibly matter today if nuns are good news or bad? Since I
am fool enough to ask this question, what do I, personally,
really believe?

I believe in a God who is utterly other, and yet in whom
we live and move and have our being. He is at once immanent
and transcendent, one and three-personed, inexpressible and
self-revealing. I believe that we human beings, perhaps the
only self-reflecting creatures in the universe, not only seem to
be made for an end too good for us, as Plato described it, but
were made for that end which we call God. And this God is
not out there, not at some unspecified future time, but now
and in the deepest place of our confused humanity. I believe
that among the many thousand names of the un-nameable
God, Love is the one that speaks him best. In Jesus Christ
love is tangibly the expression of God's ultimate self-revealing.
I believe that in Jesus we see God and through the Spirit of
Jesus we experience God in the whole of life. I believe that
in his life, death and resurrection we are caught up into the
break-through of creative loving which is a share of God's
life, whatever this may mean. But believing this I know myself
responsible for the power that it has given me. My way of
life may be irrelevant, but it is part of the world of today. I
touch and am touched by the reality of that world in all its
beauty and pain, in all its vulnerability and destructiveness
and heroism. Above all I touch and am touched by people.
To some of these, my congregation, I have committed myself
in a way that demands a particular kind of fidelity unto
death. Together, during the span of our lives, by loving or
withholding love, we shall have created or destroyed something of humanity, something of the world so loved by God
that he gave his only-begotten Son for its salvation. These
are words hackneyed by over use. But part of my mandate
for life is to discover their meaning in my own flesh.

In my own flesh. I am a woman committed with other
women to a way of life we would want to be for greater loving.
I believe that this commitment has more relevance than we
can measure, and that together we have something important
to say to the Church and to a world wider than the official

Church, something that only women can say because of the place in Judaeo-Christian tradition of the mystery that is woman.

The Old Testament gave us Eve, woman, and original source of temptation, the myth figure that is with us till the end of time. But the poetry of Hosea and Ezekiel equates the whole people of God to the bride, unfaithful, adulterous, but loved and reclaimed. The God of Abraham, Isaac and Jacob is a God of relationship, and his relationship with his people is one of tender love, forgiveness, compassion, best expressed in the imagery of marriage. Or, as with the explicitly sexual harem love lyrics of the Song of Songs, God is lover and beloved, and rejoices in his people as a lover rejoices in the woman loved. This is imagery dear to the mystics of all times, men and women alike. Or, again, this God has a more than mother's face in the poetry of Isaiah, who uses the human experience of the most faithful and self-transcending love we know, to say God's love is even greater.

The myth of Eve, the temptress, may be with us till the end of time, but at the crossroads of salvation history Mary, the mother of Jesus, becomes the new Eve. The early Church found in her the continuity of the myth woman, and also, in the fact of her physical motherhood, the assurance of the full humanity of her son. It was in the womb of Mary that, as the great prologue of John's Gospel says: 'The Word was made flesh, he lived among us . . .'[4] Through Mary the dream of philosophers and poets became a reality for the new people of a new covenant: the self-awareness of the God of a thousand names, who revealed himself as the bridegroom of Israel, now lives as man. The Divine is fully human, so that all humanity might be divine.

As the new people of the new covenant, men and women shared a fullness of fellowship. Before the day of Pentecost, we are told, the apostles were persevering in one mind in prayer with the women and Mary the mother of Jesus, waiting for the promised Spirit.[5] Time has eroded the impact of what this meant in the revolution that Christianity was for women. The early Church, reflecting on the teaching of the Lord in the light of its own experience as community, makes much of

---

[4] John 1:14.
[5] cf. Acts 1:14.

his extraordinary contacts with women, who have a place in
the synoptic Gospels out of all proportion to their place in
the Jewish society of the time. Their inclusion as full members
of the new-born Church through the initiation ceremony of
baptism was apparently unquestioned. This was remarkable
in a world where the good Jew thanked God he was not a
woman, and where the question of the retention of the all-
male initiation ceremony of circumcision became a matter of
such argument.

The people of the new covenant, like the people of the old,
are personified as Woman. In the poetic prophecy of the Book
of Revelation, the Gospel parable of the kingdom as marriage
feast culminates in the image of the Church, the New Jerusalem, as the bride adorned for her husband.

The teaching of Paul tells us again and again that each
Christian baptized into the death of Christ is alive with his
Spirit. Each Christian, now no longer Jew or gentile, male or
female, slave or free,[6] is offered a resurrection life even in the
here and now of suffering mortality. The Church, the whole
community of believers, is described as Bride and as Body in
Paul's attempt to put into words the indissolubility of this
union. John, writing later, makes the last of the 'I am' statements of Jesus, 'I am the vine'.[7] Bride, Body, Vine are three
powerful metaphors for the union of 'Mother Church', the
community of individual Christians, with Christ their Lord.

John, the last of the New Testament writers, makes a
further link in symbolism which is important to the theme of
the mystery that is woman in the tradition of the people of
God. John's Gospel places the marriage feast of Cana at the
beginning of the public ministry of Jesus. Mary is present
with dramatic significance and initiates the first great Sign,
even before her Son feels that 'his hour' has come. At the
consummation of that ministry, when his hour is come and
he is crucified, John shows her standing by the cross. There,
at the bidding of Jesus she becomes the mother of all who
are to be reborn in him. Mary, not Eve, is now the mother
of the living; Mary the woman, in the darkness of faith and
the ordinariness of the human condition, is identified with
the Bride, the Church.

[6]   cf. Galatians 3:28.
[7]   John 15.

The revolutionary wholeness of humanity experienced by the Church in its beginnings was, as we know, short-lived. Gnosticism, refuted by the early Church, was only the first heresy born of dualistic thinking to strike at the root of Christian incarnational faith. In all their different disguises, the plausible abstractions that make sense of our human experience of being spirit trapped in body, end by distorting the vision of one Christ alive in his followers. The community of believers may resist contamination at the level of formulated belief, but the matter versus spirit, body versus soul interpretation of human awareness is insidious, and it is a short step from this dualism to the conclusion that the body is evil and the soul good, or at least to the conclusion that the soul is important and the body is not. It is, after all, not so very long since the priest, giving the Catholic communicant the host, would pray that 'the body of Christ keep your soul to life everlasting'.

Clearly, from this dualism grew the condemnation of the flesh, the down-grading of marriage as, at its best, a 'better to marry than to be tortured'[8] option for the Christian less whole-heartedly seized by Christ. Real woman is back again in the role of Eve the temptress and, though 'she will be saved by childbearing',[9] she is seen over against the ideal woman, Mary, and those consecrated virgins and widows who have renounced the flesh and are increasingly over-idealized and separated from ordinary life.

The Church, the *ecclesia*, was still the Bride without spot or wrinkle, but instead of being understood as the whole people of the new covenant it became more and more an abstract idea, made present to the faithful by a centralized authority, a sacrilized bureaucracy, the quasi-magic power of priesthood, with consecrated virginity as one of its most powerful symbols. What a caricature! Or is it?

We have now refound the meaning of Church as 'the people of God', and we have witnessed the insistence in Vatican II that Mary the mother of Jesus be given her place within, not apart from, the Church. But for how many of us does the image of either St Peter's, Rome, or a local building with a steeple come to the mind as we say the word 'Church'? It is

8   1 Corinthians 7:9.
9   1 Timothy 2:15.

perhaps not without significance that the ancient rite of the consecration of virgins and that of the consecration of a local church have such strong liturgical resemblance. Both underline the presence of the sacred versus the secular, another dualistic concept.

If then we are to rediscover the wholeness of the true 'ecclesia', the community of believers who have one heart and one mind, we must rediscover the place of woman in the Church. We, the nuns, may feel that we have been idealized, sacrilized and dehumanized, but we have had, and have, our recognized place. We are all too clearly a mirror of the Church with which we have been identified. There was a time when we looked into that mirror with great satisfaction. Today, as we recognize the distortion, we must take the reponsibility of restoring the true reflection so that men and women, leading single lives or vowed in celibate or married chastity, may know themselves to be a people consecrated by baptism as body and bride of Christ.

This is where we started. It does not matter in the world today if nuns are good news or bad, but if the Church is to rediscover a Gospel wholeness it matters immeasurably if women are good news or bad, and nuns make up a very large number of searching and self-aware women.

2.   Call

If the word 'Church' brings certain immediate images to the mind which afterthought repudiates, so does the word 'vocation', at least to the Roman and Anglo-Catholic. The difference is perhaps that afterthought would not necessarily change the image of vocation, which is less a picture than a presumption. For the Evangelical of whatever persuasion the word would be, more probably, 'call' and would have a less organizational connotation, but both terms obviously have their origin in Jesus' call to his disciples to follow him, to be with him. For the Christian then, there is one vocation: to be Christian. The implications of all that the new life in Christ offers and demands must be discovered by each of the baptized in response to this first and greatest vocation.

But Scripture and the experience of the early Church does imply a further call of God. 'Further', or 'deeper', or 'more immediate' are misleading words, and once again imply a 'holier than . . .', 'better than . . .' concept of measurement which bedevils this whole area. By baptism all are called to be holy unto God, as God himself is holy, not through muscle-power, but through the acceptance of a created share in the fullness of being that is God himself. The way in which this is lived out day by day must be a matter of search. 'The 'Godspell' setting of Richard of Chichester's prayer comes to mind. Every Christian must sing in his or her heart: 'One thing I pray – to know thee more clearly, to love thee more dearly, and to follow thee more nearly.'

And like it or not, this is going to mean for some a more radical commitment to an immediate being with and for the Lord. The result may not be a 'holier than' or a 'better than'. No one will ever know in this world. But the experience is of ineluctable choice. In the Old Testament this experience was always accompanied by a sense of inescapability, and was also always for a special work. The one chosen was in some way responsible for furthering God's saving power or was called to speak the word that burned in the heart to a people who had lost heart, or to challenge the injustice by which the people were oppressed and exploited. In the New Testament Jesus calls some to be with him in a way that makes the early Church replace the lost member, Judas, by Matthias, recognizing that there was a special place within the group for this particular witness of close followers. Many later followers of the way have found the Holy Spirit speaking through something as fragile as the drawing of straws in deciding what was momentous. For Saul of Tarsus, however, a more dramatic encounter with the risen Christ was needed, and that too has had its re-enactment throughout the history of Christendom.

The one constant factor is that for each one so called, so touched by the inexpressible reality of the action of God, there seems to be a purpose, not so much a 'Why', though that is part of the mystery, but a 'What for', a work to be done in the name of his whole people. Here again, Mary the Mother of Jesus stands in the place of greatest significance. Her call was inward, inexpressible, inexplicable. The result of her assent might have been death by stoning, or at least divorce and public shame. Her life continued in the darkness of faith and in a mystery which asked only that she go on going on in the way that women somehow manage to do. We know the end of the story. She did not know it, and her greatest gift to all humanity was that she 'treasured all these things, and pondered them in her heart',[1] saying 'yes' to a now which only hindsight showed to be the presence of the longed-for kingdom. It is good to keep in mind her woman-hood and her rootedness in the commonplace as we think now, not of the image of the Church, but of the mystery that is vocation.

The purpose of this book is to look at the revolution in religious thinking of the forty years of my own experience, and vocation is its door. For me it goes back a long way farther than forty years, but it holds two things together, my own story and the way in which this unfolded in a particular social and ecclesiastical climate.

---

[1] Luke 2:19.

It is said that it is always the 'story' that matters. In this question of vocation, what is my story, and who am I that I can say to an initial call or to the call of today, 'Here I am, since you called me'.[2] This, then, is my account of my vocation. No matter how much it is demythologized it remains a mystery.

I am, and always have been, a spoilt brat. My mother and father married in October 1914 after some years of being in love. My father, a professional soldier and the son of a professional soldier, was too proud to ask my mother to marry him until he felt he had something to offer her. The result was that they waited to marry until the first year of the war, which separated them almost immediately. My brother David was born in 1916 and I was born five years later in India and grew up with far too much attention paid to my slightest wish in my almost only-child status. Part of my love and admiration for my brother is for his patient kindness and unshakeable friendship for a sister whom he must have wanted to murder, and who certainly got away with murder increasingly as the years went on and our parents grew farther apart. Looking back at my childhood I have an enormous gratitude: to each of our parents for their unconditional loving of us both and for being the people that they were; to my brother for his readiness to descend to my level and play with me; and for the earliest years when we were still very much a family. I am grateful that I feel I belong to no one world and to no one place. A Scottish regiment in which my grandfather, my father and eventually my brother served was a sort of mobile home, and somewhere in the background were my mother's country roots and the stage and musical connections. For my mother and father there were always friends, friends and more friends. There were also relations by the dozen. My grandmothers belonged to families of sixteen and ten brothers and sisters respectively, and so exciting/insane/titled/much-married/much-divorced/scandalous and virtuous great-uncles and aunts abounded and produced a network of more or less distant cousins to be claimed or discarded at will.

My background was strictly ecumenical and my first awareness of denominational difference came when I was five. Our nomadic existence took us at that time to Stirling, the depot

2 1 Samuel 3:4.

of the regiment. One day when out for a walk with Ann, who is one of the major wisdom-figures of my life and the greatest friend any of us ever had, we met the local minister. My memory is imprinted by his splendid black moustache which established an immediate denominational difference. Priests and parsons, known by dog collars, did not have moustaches. He stopped us and after some polite preliminaries asked why we had not been seen in the kirk. Ann stiffened, and drawing herself up to her full five-foot-one said that the two children and their mother were Roman Catholics, the Major was Episcopalian and she was Church of England – but we were all going to heaven by different roads. We then swept off, heads held high. For ever in my mind there has remained a comforting picture of heaven, with its walls very properly of jasper, perched on a hilltop, and a veritable spaghetti-junction of ascending individualized roads leading to its pearly gates.

Ann was always important to the God side of my life. My mother heard my prayers and taught mind-expanding new ones like the Hail Mary. But Ann always walked and talked with God and had a Scripture quotation for every occasion. I never now see dogs panting impatiently for a walk or a cat looking reproachfully at an empty saucer without murmuring to myself, 'How long, O Lord, how long?' But Ann's God was comparatively free of churches, though she and I had some disastrous experiments into the business of church-going when my mother was away.

One such I have described in the prologue. The circus-going conclusion to that story was typical of our lives. We seemed, in fact, to be a sort of travelling circus, and wherever we went a menagerie went with us. Ann's capacity for making unlikely animals friends with each other was only equalled by her capacity for unbending butlers when we were banished for a statutory visit to some grand house. 'The lion and the lamb lie down together' was the scripture text for a basket in the nursery in which a dog, a cat and its kittens, and at one time a bantam cock and a rabbit, would be cuddled together. This was not so much a pious comment as a command, and was usually accompanied by the sort of look that would have made any lion, wolf, or bear instantaneously vegetarian. The butlers did not evoke anything memorably biblical.

The business of falling in love is also important in my story. I cannot remember with whom I fell in love first. Possibly it was the Blue Bell Fairy in *The Flower Fairy Book*. Certainly during the Isle of Wight period of our lives and therefore at about three plus I loved our batman, Private Knock, with an absorbing passion. A sense of the immense burden of this loving came over me one day during breakfast. The feeling is linked in my memory with 'Force', that early brand of cornflakes which had Sunny Jim striding off the cardboard of the packet. I knew that I could not eat those cornflakes without letting Knock know just how much I loved him. Somehow his reply to this declaration, that he loved me too but at that moment loved his breakfast best, was satisfying, and a general glow of warmth made Sunny Jim for ever radiant in my heart.

Of course at that time I was in love with my father and counted on the fact that I would be left alone with him on Sunday mornings when my mother went off to Mass taking the church-going members of the household with her in our rattle-bang car. It was another proof that God and happiness had very little to do with church but a lot to do with loving.

Love, hero-worship and the conviction that I would one day be able to persuade the regiment to accept me as a recruit were the religion of my life. If I prayed with fervour it was that I might have a cold and be saved from Sunday Mass. But God was present in the hands that held me and in the dogs, cats and guinea-pigs and ponies that made up my existence. I did not see any nuns or register their existence until I was nearly ten. Then the regiment was posted to Edinburgh and I was sent to a small day-school attached to the teachers' training college at Craiglockhart run by the religious of the Society of the Sacred Heart. There I found nuns I liked, others I did not, but they did not impinge on my life as people. They were nuns. My main object was to be as unwell as possible so as not to be obliged to stay at school in the afternoons, and somehow I managed this through the four years of our Edinburgh posting. At one time when the excuse of being too delicate to cope with a full day's schooling was clearly wearing a bit thin, I remember explaining to the superior, a woman of great perspicacity, the altruistic necessity of being free to ride every afternoon for the good of my pony and my father. She showed herself convinced. May God reward her for her understanding and insight.

Religious life made its first serious impact during those years in Edinburgh not through the religious of the Sacred Heart, but through Carmel. My mother, a convert, had a deep love for Carmel, and often visited the Edinburgh Carmelite monastery. Mass at Carmel was memorable for the discomfort of the prie-dieux and the incomprehensible chanting of the invisible Carmelites. Above all I was oppressed by the general smell of cold poverty, boiled cabbage and incense, by the grilles and doors and high walls. But before we left Edinburgh when I was thirteen my mother took me with her to see the prioress who treated me as a godchild and opened the grille shutters on my side of the room, so that I could see her while we talked. She spoke very freely about life in Carmel, and made me feel adult and respected. She also gave me a brown leather copy of *The Imitation of Christ* which I still have, black-mailing me, with a promise of prayer for my mother as well as for myself, to read it daily, and marking the passage: 'love him and keep him for thy friend who when all else depart will not leave thee nor suffer thee to perish at the last'.[3] It was a promise made and kept.

It was during those four years in Edinburgh that I grew from a spoilt child to a tiresomely sophisticated spoilt adolescent. It was a time of great discovery of friendship and of course a marvellous time for falling in love with unwitting subalterns, and fantasizing about it with my friends who are still my friends today.

Most importantly, nuns had come into my life. Nothing would have persuaded me then I should ever be one myself, but their way of life had been presented to me, and the way of Carmel, which was repellent in its externals, made sense in its heroic essentials; I could see it as a way of laying down one's life for love and I was forced to admire it.

When we left Edinburgh my father had only a few months left before completing his command of the regiment, and my mother went on strike at the thought of setting up house for so short a time. We made our base at her old home and, as my brother was by this time at Sandhurst, my father moved into the Mess, and my mother and I went off to Italy for a time of blissful wandering and disorganized culture. This was probably the moment in my life when the Church as Church

---

[3]   Thomas à Kempis, *The Imitation of Christ*, Book II, Chap. 7.

became important to me. But not nuns. I was furious at being subjected to some weeks as paying guest at the glorious Fiesole convent of the Little Company of Mary instead of staying at some swinging Florentine hotel (no hope of that – we were doing our Italian journeys in third-class trains with *Italy on Ten Pounds* tucked under my mother's arm). I was even more furious when the nuns there made appreciative noises about the fact that I had been at school with the Religious of the Sacred Heart, and said that any 'child of the Sacred Heart' could be recognized anywhere. Assisi was nearly ruined for me by an American Franciscan who dealt with guests in the convent where we stayed. She fixed me with her sapphire eyes and said that a vocation was something that could be seen so clearly in a girl like me. She was lucky to have escaped with sapphire eyes unblackened. Finally spending some weeks in Rome with a musician friend of my mother's, I discovered that she had been at school at Riedenburg, a famous Sacred Heart convent in Austria. She encouraged me to call on the Sacred Heart nuns at the Trinità dei Monti. I refused with passion.

Amongst the motley crew of those with whom I had fallen in love during this Italian tour was Mrs Curry, the wife of the then headmaster of Dartington Hall. We were in Merano, in the Italian Tyrol and we were not convent-based. Our normal habit was to avoid the English as others would avoid the plague-stricken, but for some reason we linked up with her and she won my all too impressionable heart. Her descriptions of school life at Dartington Hall fitted my ideals of education, and from then on I used all the power of my manipulative arm to persuade my parents to give me my head in the co-educational experimentalism of this dream school. There I saw myself developing my genius as artist, actress, writer, but above all escaping from nuns.

But there was to be no Dartington Hall for me, and the red brick of the Convent of the Sacred Heart built in the 1870s on the Upper Drive, Hove, closed in on me in the autumn of 1935. I went miserable and rebellious, muttering that I was sewing my shroud as I marked indestructible chillpruf vests and underpants with Cash's tapes. I stayed to love every brick in the place.

The impact on me of the nuns as people was unexpected. I found them to be women of humour and sanity, and they seemed to have a purpose in life that was far bigger than the world of a girls' school. Above all, I found as Headmistress, Mother Ogilvie Forbes, with whom, after nearly fifty years, I have not yet fallen out of love. I also experienced a curious sense of home-coming. Here was a place where I belonged, where the language I spoke as a person was understood, and where there was freedom in spite of the framework of school rules. It was, oddly enough, a far greater freedom than that of the grown-up world into which I had been trespassing. Here too I found friendship, space to be myself, ideas, the challenge to do well and use my mind, and in overcoming my inherent dilettantism I discovered the excitement of achievement. Thus the spoilt brat who arrived determined to leave as soon as was decently possible, and who made it clearly known that she was far too much of a hot-house bloom to be faced with the strain of public examinations, ended by staying on a year beyond the agreed minimum and actually planning to go on to university.

The most important part of this education was the opportunity offered for prayer. The retreats, the Holy Hours before the first Fridays of the month and the great liturgies of Holy Week were doors into a relationship with God which was like finding water. It was darker and deeper water and more dangerous than I could understand, but it was water for which I was somehow thirsting.

Perhaps it was part of the theology of the time that during my last year at school I had come to want a vocation, but to feel that I had not got one. Cordelia in Evelyn Waugh's *Brideshead Revisited* treats the bewildered Charles to a description of this kind of thinking which makes the magic Call of God so special that, however much it may be desired, if you have not 'got it' then all attempts at the religious life are doomed to failure. But how does one know if one has got it? My headmistress referring to the rampant, romantic convent-schoolgirl variety of imagined vocation as the 'divine measles', saw no harm in the contagion, but gave little support to those who tried to claim the temporary malaise as the real thing.

During the Holy Week of 1939 I had an experience in prayer that has never wholly left me. The words at the opening of the great prayer of Jesus in John 17, 'Eternal life is this: to know you, the only true God, and Jesus Christ

whom you have sent',[4] leapt out of the Gospel page in a way
that overwhelmed me by its immediacy. It was an experience
of reality greater than that of any reality I had known. War,
peace, success, failure were all suddenly unimportant in the
now of eternity and of life. I do not remember telling anyone
of this experience, only of walking round the hockey field in
a world suddenly translucent to the wordless joy of the Word.
But was that a vocation? It did not seem to fit the expectation
I had that something would say to me: 'Nun'.

Then on a June morning during an Italian lesson the Lord
said, 'Nun'. I was the only pupil in the school learning Italian,
and my teacher was a gentle, scholarly graduate who seemed
to appear from outer space for the lesson and then to disappear into darkest Brighton leaving no trace behind her. For
some reason linked to her personal devotion, we were reading
a life of Catherine of Siena. It was evocative to me of the
Italian months of my unregenerate pre-boarding-school days,
and I could picture the little cell where Catherine's dialogue
with Christ took place, and the steep hill path that passed
the house and led down from the town to the valley. The
passage we were reading was the well-known one of Catherine's night of temptation. It was a modern biography and
described imaginatively Catherine, self-imprisoned and alone,
hearing the night sounds of the young people of Siena singing
and laughing together as they go down the hill to the Summer
Woods. It then moved into straight dialogue: Catherine asks
her Lord where he had been during the night hours she had
spent fighting with the flesh. He in his reply of tenderness
calls her 'Caterina figliola mia' and says that he had been
closer to her than she was to herself . . . That was the moment
of certainty. In some unknown way where Catherine had
been, I had to be.

---

[4] John 17:3.

3. Response

It was all very well knowing that I had this mysterious thing a 'vocation', a sort of indelible mark of Abel, but during the years that separated me from the noviciate I had got to find out where and to what congregation I should offer myself.

I left school in July 1939 and war offered an immediate and kaleidoscopic series of work-experiences during the years that followed. I spent some time in a Vauxhall settlement with the families of those who had returned from evacuation, and met a poverty I had never known; I worked in hospitals as a V.A.D. before and after an experience of prolonged boredom as minor clerk in M.I.5.; I made friends, fell in and out of love and shed at least some of my convent-girl priggishness.

The M.I.5. clerk period was important because during it the idea of vocation as such grew distant, looking like something seen through the wrong end of a telescope. The department was evacuated to Blenheim Palace after the bombing of its London hide-out. I happened to have the good fortune during this time to be part of a two-family take-over of the top floors of the Oxford home of Joyce Carey, the author, and his delightful wife, Trudy. The sheer interdependent warmth of Joyce and Trudy Carey's marriage partnership was a challenge to my thinking. Theirs was a family able to express its affection and mutual admiration with unselfconscious humour and intelligence. Ours was a family that hid its feelings deep, and my parents' marriage had become more and more a relationship of parallel lines. So many of the marriages around seemed to be falling apart for want of love, or holding together for the sake of appearances. Was I therefore chasing this nun-business because of my observation of the half-alive married men and women who compared unfavourably with the fully alive, tangibly fulfilled nuns who

had influenced me at school? Was I cutting out the possibility
of marriage as a way of holiness and wholeness because of a
typical convent-girl vocation fantasy of pseudo-mysticism?

Joyce Carey and a glass of sherry broke into this time of
questioning. There was some sort of party going on, whether
Carey-given or evacuee-given I do not remember. *The House
of Children* had just been published and we were talking about
the clearly autobiographical experience of the small boy 'I'.
There is the moment when he does not know to which world
he belongs – to the nursery, or out with the guns on the
morning of a shoot. No one has told him exactly what to do,
and for a moment he is a little bit insane. This led to the
discussion of the insanity of uncertainty in adult life, and for
some reason, at his direction, not mine, we were on to religious vocation. To my astonishment (had the man second
sight? I really did not think I looked like a would-be nun or
behaved like a would-be nun), I found myself hearing him
state his conviction that a true vocation and a true marriage
started from the same place – a recognition of the heart.
Somewhere or other he said: 'That's something for you from
an Irish Protestant.' I remember asking if he believed that
there was such a thing as a vocation to the religious life. His
reply as I heard it was that whether he did or did not at that
moment of his life believe in a transcendent God, he believed
in a God who was immanent. His own experience of this
immanent God could be called, for want of a better term,
relationship. For him a true religious vocation was an experience that assented, not *to* that relationship but *in* that relationship, wholly, absolutely, for better, for worse, for richer for
poorer, but for love only. I had responded inwardly to the
experience of temporary insanity in the hero of *The House of
Children*. I now responded to this with astonished certainty.

In what congregation I was to ask for admittance became
clearer a few weeks later during a visit to two of my school
friends, now members of the noviciate of the Society of the
Sacred Heart. During this visit I spoke to the Mistress of
Novices and suggested to her that probably my place should
be Carmel. I knew that she herself was a convert to Catholicism who had tried her vocation as a Poor Clare, and that
her understanding of prayer and people would help me. It
did. I have no exact idea of what she said, but she knocked
my Carmelite aspirations to the smithereens they deserved. I

suddenly realized my presumption to have been that if a nun at all then only the hardest, the highest, the most total reversal of all that was humanly pleasing, could be right for me. Without Joyce Carey's sherry party conversation, however, I doubt if I could have heard the suggestion now made that what I was looking for in Carmel was the ending of a film in which I alone walked into the sunset with the violins playing as the credits came up – the unforgettable name of Prudence Wilson against each of them.

For me, the response 'in relationship' had to be at the level of the undramatic if it were to be true, with a deep realization that with God there is no heroic giving, only an incredible receiving in poverty and in love.

I asked to be received into the Society of the Sacred Heart in the autumn of 1942 just after my twenty-first birthday, but for various reasons there was no chance of entering the noviciate until the following May. As soon as the letter accepting me for the Society came, however, so did total blackness. The fact that this is not unusual does not lessen the pain of the sufferer. Quite apart from the excellent arguments which I could put to myself about self-deception and the unreality of my imagined experience of God, there was the clear Christian reproach of sheer selfishness. My mother would be left alone in a war-torn world, with my father fighting his part of it in Ethiopia and my brother in Burma. How could I leave her to face the possible news of the death of either or both of them simply to fulfil my own pious whim? Then to make matters worse I found myself telling her that to enter was the very last thing in the world I wanted to do but I just knew I had to do it. How can an unfortunate mother handle that piece of lunacy, especially when the blame for the whole thing was being laid at her door in weekly letters from my hurt, angry, bewildered father? She was seen to be the Roman Catholic convert, the nun-loving, daily Mass-going, undermining influence of my otherwise healthy young life.

Then of course, predictably, I had to fall in love again, this time it seemed, seriously. I am sorry for the pain I gave by my clumsiness and inability to put my blind panic into words, but for my own pain I am grateful. Something of understanding of the vocation to marriage or to celibacy for the sake of the kingdom came from it that could never otherwise have come so personally. On my way to a party one evening

I had about an hour to spare and I slipped into a church. It seemed to me then, in spite of the fog of my prayer, that there was an open way before me, either to go on my journey to God together with another, or alone. Both could be ways of holiness, and God seemed to say to me 'choose'. And I saw again that the choice was already made. At least I thought it was made and that what I had seen was final clarification. It was enough for the next stage of the journey and, although the total darkness that came with acceptance by the Society remained with me before and after the actual process of entering, there was always a sense of being carried, and a strength and sureness in the God who carried me. However, no permission from whatever national authority I had to apply to for release from war work had come in time for me to enter on the day I had planned, May 25th. This is the feast of the foundress of the Society, St Madeleine Sophie Barat, and it seemed a suitable date. I therefore asked the Mistress of Novices for a further week's grace and went to the necessary office to find out why there had been no reply to my written application. Feeling more of a fool than usual, I spoke to a lady behind a desk. She was sympathetic and courteously uninquisitive, though I detected a quiver of kindly pity when, swallowing hard, I stated that my reason for asking for release was to become a nun. I also said that it was important for me to know the answer on the 25th. In fact it was not, but the date gave me further opportunity to test the Lord my God in a way that was becoming almost shock-proof. ('Lord, if you really want me to be a nun, give me the chance of riding again', was one of the many spoilt-brat demands for reassurance, each of which he had answered in kind.) Now it was: 'If you really want me to enter, give me the answer by May 25th. If not, then I shall go and sign up at a proper nursing school and see what life brings when I am trained.'

In those far-off days of many postal deliveries, no word of my release came through, even by the last post of May 25th. Privately congratulating myself and God, I felt that at 8 p.m. I was safe to telephone a friend and go off to celebrate. As I reached for the 'phone it rang instead, and the sympathetic, uninquisitive but compassionate voice of the lady behind the desk asked for me, personally. She said she had taken it upon herself to contact me from her own home as the date had seemed so important. She felt I would be glad to know that the letter of release was in the post. However as it could not yet have reached me, she wanted to tell me herself, on the day I had given, that I was free to enter 'my' convent. I hope I sounded grateful. I did not ring the friend and I did not celebrate, but I could not reproach God. He was obviously still in charge.

Benedict, the practical visionary who set a pattern for the following of Christ through consecration to his service lived out in community, has one question for the would-be monk who presents himself at the monastery: 'Do you truly seek God?' Thereafter as much discouragement as possible is advised to prove the sincerity of the 'postulant', or one who asks admission. I had a long way still to go in answering that question when, on the evening of May 31st 1943, having missed as many train connections as possible, I eventually walked through the door of the noviciate. It happened to be a stable door.

We were a small noviceship group, housed for the war in part of the stable block of what is now a 'stately home', Stanford Hall near Rugby. For the first four months I was the only postulant. I came expecting far more than the considerable physical hardship I found, but I was totally unprepared for the psychological shock and intense bewildering bereavement that submerged me. Did I truly seek God, and what was this God asking of me? The words of Thomas More, written to his daughter Meg, were an anchor to me at that time: 'Mistrust him will I not, though I feel me faint.' I wrote to my former headmistress, Mother Ogilvie Forbes, who had been so important in my search for God's will, that my one prayer was, 'Five minutes more, dear Lord, and then I pack my toothbrush'. The reply came, 'Three cheers for God and the toothbrush'. It was some time before I could answer, 'Amen'.

Nothing in all this is extraordinary. Many others have felt as I did, and have described the experience with all the rueful self-mockery that one feels as one looks back over the years at the misery of the beginnings. What, in fact, had all this bereavement, this way of reversing human values and cutting oneself off from the normal ties of family and friends to do with God, with Jesus, who until his passion did not seem to live a life remote from the ordinary?

'Do you truly seek God?' For some he is the God of the absolute, and he will show himself such, no matter how outwardly mitigated the way of life in a religious community may be. For my generation, and for many that followed afterwards, the one pattern of noviciate, not only in the orders and congregations of men and women, but also in the seminaries of secular priests, was monastic. Age-old customs, the relevance of which had been lost hundreds of years before most of our congregations adopted them, were the accepted, tried and symbolically satisfying way of stating our choice to seek God. Everything about the way we lived was intended to show that our guide in our actions was faith not reason. Though the two have not necessarily to be opposed, the transcendence of God seems to demand a gesture of adoration. If God is God, then he far surpasses reason, and all that reason can say about him is that total folly may be the best and only way to declare faith in his otherness. For me personally this was a good way and perhaps a necessary way. I am glad, however, that it is not the way of today in its outward demands. The inward will always be there.

At that time, physical hardship was the least of the experiences of rupture with a former way of life for the newcomer. Most of us expected something far more exciting, and were reminded that the way of the Society was low-key and undramatic. We got up at 5.20, a concession to wartime conditions. But as five past ten was the time for 'lights out' some of us who had been enjoying life before we entered had rather more sleep than usual. Meals were institutional, wartime, but adequate, and prepared with love. The fact that only one plate was used, cleaned between courses with a piece of bread, seemed to me the height of imaginative economy, and I decided I would sell it to my family and friends as the idea of the century.

We worked hard, but the work was necessary and real. I was almost immediately into the business of tree-felling and wood-stacking and sawing, and enjoyed it. Prayer was demanding, reading and study well-directed, and the daily instruction on the constitutions and spirit of the institute obviously what we were all about.

Less trivial was the fact that we were strictly enclosed, and that although with permission parents and friends might come to see us, we knew that we would never again see our homes, and we knew that we would not, for example, be able to visit a dying parent. We could not write home, even to parents, without knowing that the letter would be read. This would continue for the rest of our lives, not simply for the time of noviceship. It was a limitation on freedom and privacy at a deep level, but I had voluntarily put my neck under this yoke and I was not rebelling against the demands of the life as I wept my way through the first few months of my postulantship. There was certainly a sense of inward death in this loss of privacy which the kindness, fairness and openness with which the system was applied, could not mitigate. I had wanted something radical, and this was more radical than any physical hardship.

At a far deeper level there was bereavement in the lost hope of sexual fulfilment and of motherhood. Once again this was a deliberate choice, freely entered into because of the realization that for me the way to God was a way alone, but everything in me cried out in rebellion. The normal young man or woman must rebel against choosing to be an eunuch[1] for the sake of the kingdom, and it is better that the rebellion be conscious and furious than that it be sublimated and unacknowledged, only to surface later to take its revenge.

But for me this bereavement was at the centre of my conscious pain, diminishing even the hardship, homesickness and loss of personal privacy. I wrestled in the dark with a God who was no longer there to be wrestled with, inwardly shouting at his deafness. If he would let me escape from this life-sentence I would have seventeen children all of whom could be priests and nuns if he wanted. The string of names I used as I practised a form of traditional calligraphy, was in fact, a variation of the possible names and sexes of those seventeen children and the prayer with which I wrote them was to tell God in his absence that he had made me for life not death.

Whether he was absent or present, he was God. I had no doubt of that, and if he had got me so far he alone must show me the next step of the journey. But my obedience to a vocation might be that of Abraham with my angry body playing the role of Isaac. Perhaps God would ask me to take it to the place of sacrifice, and there give me a reprieve? Once

[1] cf. Matthew 19:12.

again I decided to set a date, and test this God of patience and compassion. The community and noviceship retreat began on August 19th. This would be the top of the mountain and in some miraculous way a ram would be found and Isaac would be free. I was not a great believer in novenas but there was a crumpled bit of typescript in my office book which declared itself 'efficacious'. It was to St Francis Xavier, a saint I knew little about. I had no idea when his feast was, nor whether this was important to the efficacy of the novena. With all the superstitious fervour of desperation I made that novena, not just for nine days, but nine times daily from August 10th. On the 19th, with no sign of a substitute sacrifice, we started our retreat, and telling St Francis Xavier what I thought about him, I threw the typescript novena into the paperbasket.

'Do you truly seek God'? Yes, in spite of the darkness and rebellion, in spite of the pain of bereavement, then, as in many later times in life, I knew the only thing that made sense was for me to seek him. It was therefore in that frame of mind that I went into the first eight-day retreat I had ever made and God was there again, deeply and peacefully present, saying nothing, but no longer a God of darkness and deafness. Then three things happened, the first a preparation for the second, and the third its confirmation.

The Mistress of Novices suggested to me that I return in great trust and freedom to what had seemed to me to be the original moment of clarification of my vocation. St Catherine of Siena and the Italian lesson were part of another life, but when I looked again at the whole incident it had a meaning far more in tune with where I was in August 1943 than in June 1939. I knew far better what the sense of being cut off felt like as the laughing crowd of friends went on their way down to the summer woods, and I knew something of what it was to wrestle with my sexuality as a woman. Then as I stood by a carved crucifix in the noviceship, the text of the epistle of John came to me, 'He gave up his life for us, and we too ought to give up our lives for our brothers'.[2] The inner rebellion stopped. There was not going to be a substitute sacrifice. There was no substitute sacrifice on Calvary. What I was being asked was to be one heart with Jesus, in life, in death, 'for the brethren'. I did not know what that meant,

[2] 1 John 3:16.

but I knew once again the call to an inner assent which I was free to give or to withhold. Once again I knew that in an overwhelming offered love there can only be a 'yes'.

As the end of the retreat there was a ceremony of final profession of two who were then 'co-adjutrix' sisters. Both were, and have become more and more deeply through the years, my sisters, my friends, and always my benefactresses. The ceremony included a dialogue between them and the officiating priest. It was formalized, but very powerful. After asking to be admitted to final profession in the society, and declaring that she asks it freely, the aspirant replies to a final question: 'Do you accept Jesus Christ crucified as your spouse?' 'Yes, with all my heart.' I made my final profession on that day in the secret of my heart, but I knew that I had not chosen Jesus Crucified. I had said 'Yes, with all my heart' to his incredible choice of me.

The Mistress of Novices, Mother Margaret Shepherd, told me that she had decided to send me home if, by the beginning of September there had been no change in my rebellious struggle, no lifting of the darkness. But I was at peace, and through a series of coincidences, the date on which I was to take the habit, become a novice rather than a postulant, was fixed for December 3rd. It was the first Friday of the month, a day always held in special honour because of its connection with the cult of the Sacred Heart and chosen for the sake of a novice who was to make her first vows, and whose ceremony I was to share. It also happened to be the feast of St Francis Xavier. Two years later it was the date of my own first vows. Perhaps novenas really are 'efficacious'?

4. Outside Inside

The story of vocation has got the reluctant postulant into the noviceship and has confirmed the fact that she is there to stay. I said in the first chapter that I wanted to share a personal experience of evolution and revolution within myself and in the congregation to which I belonged. So far the sharing has been of personal evolution only, an introduction to who I am and why I am a nun. Now it seems important to introduce the congregation to which I belong, and in whose post-Vatican-II revolution I have shared. For reasons of simplification I will from now on refer to this congregation as 'the Society of the Sacred Heart' or more shortly 'the Society' knowing that in this context we shall not be confused with the Society of Jesus from whom, I think, we adopted this manner of referring to ourselves.

As a school girl and as a young religious I found in the Society of the Sacred Heart a congregation already evolved. If consecrated virginity was, and is, one of the most powerful symbols of the Church, I could see the Society symbolizing a certain aspect of the Church very powerfully. It was a microcosmic mirror in which a certain face of the Church was reflected with its contradictions and aspirations, its beauty and it woundedness. Importantly, it was the face of 'Mother Church'.

The Society of the Sacred Heart, this microcosmic reflection, was 'born' in France in 1800, in the aftermath of a revolution that shattered accepted religious values. This was the beginning of a century of enormous growth in numbers of congregations of men and women. Many of these congregations were founded because of a new awareness of social deprivation, and their members were dedicated to serve where a perceived need called them. Others, and the Society of the Sacred Heart is amongst them, seemed to grow from a 'seed of contemplation', and a work that fitted the contemplative vision then presented itself and became the outward expression of the inner call to prayer as a way of life.

The terminology used in categorizing religious orders and congregations until Vatican II was that of the 'contemplative', the 'active' and the 'mixed life'. The members of the Society for various reasons, the least important of which was canonical, would have been described as leading the 'mixed life'. An order as venerable as the Dominicans would also have described their life in these terms, and Aquinas himself, understandably for a son of St Dominic, claimed that it was a way of life most like that of Jesus.

A young priest, the Abbé de Tournély, conceived the idea which eventually came to birth as the Society of the Sacred Heart. He had studied for the priesthood at the Oratorian seminary of St Sulpice and was ordained at the beginning of the French Revolution. Together with a group of friends from the seminary, he formed an unofficial congregation and adopted the Constitutions of the Society of Jesus which was at that time suppressed by the Church. They called themselves the Fathers of the Sacred Heart, taking the description of the first Christian community 'One heart and one mind' as their motto to which they added the phrase, 'in the Heart of Jesus'.

In January 1796 Léonor de Tournély was led in prayer to believe that a parallel congregation for women with the same name and the same motto must be founded. It was to be devoted to the Sacred Heart; its aim: 'to awaken the love of Jesus in souls, and the light of his teaching in minds. For this it will enter into the sentiments and interior dispositions of the divine Heart, and will reveal them to others by means of education.'

It is important to keep the historical setting of all this in mind. These young priests faced death; the Society of Jesus to which they felt called was proscribed, not by revolutionary France but by the Church itself, and the symbol of the Sacred Heart and 'devotion' to it were under attack. The seed of contemplation was therefore planted in times of danger and of instability.

Meanwhile in 1795 Madeleine Sophie Barat, the youngest child of a Burgundian artisan, had come to Paris with her brother, a young priest who had just escaped the guillotine after months of imprisonment. He had been her tutor during her childhood and had given her a tough classical education, 'ridiculous' for a girl of her social class and expectations. Now he insisted on having her with him in Paris where, with a few friends, she lived a life of prayer and continued study, and undertook the instruction of some children from the district. Sophie had never seen nuns, but had dreamed of the life of a Carmelite. The fate of the Carmelites of Compiègne, going singing to the scaffold, must have been an inspiration to someone who could write later in her life, 'I love the heroic; there at least one has room'.

Guided by her brother in the ways of renunciation and prayer, the room for the Spirit which Sophie found was in adoration before the Blessed Sacrament in a secret oratory near their apartment. There the 'primordial idea' of the Society of the Sacred Heart came to her. Closed churches, blasphemy, political murder, anti-religious propaganda, desecration of the Eucharist, and a realization of the distortion of the truth forced upon the minds and hearts of children were the background of her prayer.

Her vision was to establish a little community which would 'adore, night and day, the Heart of Jesus, outraged in his eucharistic love'. Twenty-four religious replacing one another in turn on a prie-dieu, that would be 'much and yet so little'. 'If we had young people whom we formed to have a spirit of adoration and reparation, that would be different.' Then she widened her horizon:

> I saw hundreds, thousands of adorers before the monstrance, ideal universal, lifted high above the Church. That is it, I said . . . we must dedicate ourselves to the education of youth, rebuild in souls the firm foundation of a living faith in the Blessed Sacrament . . . we shall bring up a host of adorers of all nations, as far as the ends of the earth.[1]

How the dream of de Tournély and Sophie Barat fused, and how the Fathers of the Sacred Heart eventually found their way into the Society of Jesus when it was re-established, thus leaving the realization of the original vision to the 'parallel order of women', is part of the history of the foundation of the congregation. When I was a schoolgirl this story was part

---

[1] Quoted in Mère Perdrau, *Les Loisirs de l'Abbaye* (1934), Vol. 1, p. 423.

of our lives. Madeleine Sophie Barat, canonized ten years before I went to the boarding school at Brighton, was of course the central character of the story, and a very attractive one. The account of her dream of the Society meant that as schoolgirls, we were part of a world-embracing way of prayer and adoration. The original desire of the foundress for perpetual adoration of the Blessed Sacrament, an ideal that belonged to the period and was carried out by several congregations founded in the nineteenth century, had in fact, proved inappropriate for the Society. There were, of course, days when the Blessed Sacrament was exposed for adoration[2] and we knew that this was done daily in houses of noviceship and at the Mother House in Rome. But far more important for us was the centrality of the Mass in the life of the community and in our lives. The Eucharist always recalled us to the 'primordial vision' of the Society.

The Eucharist was, therefore, central to my apprehension of the Society from outside. Time is a strange thing, and it is difficult to believe that Saint Pius X's call to frequent communion was as near to my childhood as Vatican II is to the Church of today. The effect of the Pius X reforms in the liturgy and the rediscovery of plain-chant linked our school days closely to the liturgical movement in the Church of the period. But above all the liturgy was the setting for the Eucharist and the expressions of devotion that sprang from it. Years later, when I read the account of Teilhard de Chardin's 'vision' while he knelt in adoration before the Blessed Sacrament exposed, and it seemed to him that the Host grew till it encompassed all created things, I recognized in this my image of the Society. It was half-linked with the story of the dream of both de Tournély and of the young Sophie Barat, but it was also expressive of my sense that the lives that influenced me were lives transformed, and that they were transformed eucharistically.

As a schoolgirl I had an impression of being surrounded by women who looked towards the Lord and were radiant.[3]

[2]   Exposition of the Blessed Sacrament is the practice of placing a large consecrated host in a 'monstrance' so that it is visible to the congregation. It was seen to be a prolongation of the elevation of the Host at the consecration of the Mass. Surrounded by lights and flowers, the Host is the object of special adoration.
[3]   cf. Psalm 34.

They represented a wide spectrum of background, education, nationality, and age, but there was a bond of purpose between them which was as important to the old, the simple, or the sick, as it was to the authority-figures or to the young and active. It would be difficult to say how to define that purpose, but it was something at the level of a faith which challenged mere usefulness. It was an almost tangible realization of the motto 'one heart and one mind in the Heart of Jesus', left to the Society as a legacy from Abbé de Tournély's dream.

For those who suffered either from divine measles or from the sheer interest of belonging to such an international family, there were lives to be read of those who made up the Society's history. They were impressive and increased the number of women of vision with whom we seemed to be linked. The most interesting of these was Mother Janet Erskine Stuart, a gifted convert to Roman Catholicism, who died as Superior General of the Society in 1914. Her writings were inspirational, and long after the 1930s her biography was as much read by Anglican religious and lay men and women, as by Roman Catholics.

Mother Stuart fascinated me, and what the Society looked like from the outside was strongly coloured by her writings. Her last book, written during the long sea voyage to Australia as Mother General in 1913 and printed the day after her death at the age of fifty-seven in 1914, is her 'character sketch' of the Society of the Sacred Heart as she then perceived it.

Rereading this 'little book of the sea' I recognize the Society as I saw it from the outside and as I experienced it when I entered. The description of the 'mixed life' which Mother Stuart gives in her chapter on the 'type' is masterly:

Religious leading the mixed life, have to give proof of something that belongs to both worlds, the unseen and the seen, and a certain stress of intensity cannot fail to be the result. Towards God, the contemplative side, and towards others, the fully active, have to be awake to be affirmed and to be expressed . . . the inner life holds the key of each, and the two meet together in the quiet place of community which has its frontiers on the one side and on the other.[4]

---

[4] Janet Erskine Stuart, *The Society of the Sacred Heart* (Roehampton Press 1914), p.111.

No one can guess what might have happened if Mother Stuart had lived to carry the Society into the post-1918 world. She would not have been tied blindly to the traditional even if she might have been strongly restrained by *pietas*. The fact that her last written work was a picture of what existed may well have blocked the exploration of change which should have been taking place in the years between the wars, and even more in the years after 1945. If this was so, it was not her fault. She called her book a 'true picture, though a fleeting one . . . thankful for the past and hopeful for the future, striving in the present to realize the purpose for which it has come into being'. It was her successors who canonized the 'fleeting' picture and made it triumphantly static. But then, in so many ways the Church did exactly that. We, in the Society of the Sacred Heart, believed that a wide missionary expansion was movement as we repeated the identical model of our religious institutions all over the world. But that is exactly what the Church was doing and had done for centuries.

There is one question that I must answer for my own satisfaction before looking at the difference between the somewhat romanticized society seen from the outside and the Society that I met within. Why did I think of no other order or congregation than the Society of the Sacred Heart, or Carmel, especially after I had seen that for me to enter Carmel was a self-promoting fantasy?

When I told my brother that I was accepted for the Society of the Sacred Heart he wrote me a straight challenge: he had escaped from Singapore and was then fighting in the long Burma campaign. Here was I, at this brutal moment of history, sloping off to a way of life that perhaps had a certain austerity, but which was of no value whatever to the war effort and very little value to those in any sort of real need. He wrote of his admiration for the Little Sisters of the Poor. If I wanted to be a nun, there at least was a life that stood for something real and something Gospel.

And he was right. But the thought of linking usefulness to what I felt I was called to, never crossed my mind, unless it was the usefulness of being where Christ was for me. To enter was as useless as marriage. I may have been a prig but it would not have occurred to me for example to measure the suitability of a husband according to the amount of service to a needy world that life with him might open for my gifts and generosity. Eventually I would come to see the expression of the usefulness I was searching for in the words of St John of the Cross when he speaks of the moment of great abandonment experienced by Jesus: 'It was then he wrought the greatest work of his whole life of miracles and wonders, the reconciliation and reunion with God by grace of all mankind.'⁵ Then I had not got the words, but where Christ was I had to be, and where I had found him was in the place where he had first found me. What I did after that was his business if the purpose of it was in a mysterious way one with the 'work' of crucifixion.

But the question raises again the whole matter of sign and symbol and its misinterpretation, or right interpretation, better judged from the outside than from within. The symbol of the Little Sister of the Poor or the Daughter of Charity or the Sister of Mercy was clear in the context of the Church of the time, and so was the symbol of the Carmelite or Poor Clare. The one was of the good works of the Gospel, the other was of the folly of the Cross. The famous 'mixed life' of the Society of the Sacred Heart, which from the outside I saw clearly as the folly of the Cross lived in a way that was ordinary, undramatic, demanding, but human, looked to many people élitist and arrogant. 'The proud daughters of humble Mother Barat' was one description of 'les Dames du Sacré Coeur', dating from early in the nineteenth century.

Disraeli spoke of the two nations that made up the Britain of his day. There were two Roman Catholic Churches in the Britain of my childhood. There was the Church of the intellectuals and converts, and by and large this Church was reflected by the religious orders and congregations involved in secondary and tertiary education. At the top of this league would be those which ran good independent schools for girls or public schools for boys. Then there was the Church of the parishes, the Church which had not lost touch with the working class, because many of its greatest priests and bishops came from that class. The idea of 'vocation' within these two Churches has a different flavour. The vocation of a secular priest was often nourished by education from the age of eleven in a junior seminary and could be more pragmatic than the

⁵ *Ascent of Mt Carmel*, Book. II, Ch. 7.

vocation of the priest-religious. Above all the Catholic parish of the working-class world of the 1930s was a true community just because it was often led by priests who knew what life was really like for the unemployed and underpaid, and whose vocation was the practical Christ-response to the need of those to whom they ministered.

The women religious who shared that life were usually free from the rules of strict enclosure. They came out from the security of their convents, and in hospitals and orphanages, in homes for 'fallen girls', in reformatories and above all in parish schools, served the poor and helped build up the local church. They held up the microcosmic mirror to the Church and the reflection in it was the caring, healing, teaching face of the Bride.

The Society of the Sacred Heart, however, in spite of Saint Madeleine Sophie's insistence that a school for the poor be attached to every boarding school, and teaching in it be the one employment for which a religious of the Sacred Heart could ask, became more and more identified with the middle and upper classes.

So the face of the Church reflected in the mirror that was the Society was the Church of the intellectuals and converts, the Church of the professions and, to a certain extent, the Church of the landed gentry and aristocracy. It was an image determined by the fairly small number of families whose daughters were educated in the boarding schools and not by the families of the far greater number whose daughters were educated in the training colleges or maintained schools.

The Church of the converts and intellectuals was snobbish and exclusive; it was a Church of privilege, but it was also an exciting church, and we who were at the receiving end of the education offered by the Society of the Sacred Heart in the late 1930s were delighted to belong to it. It was the Church of Chesterton and Belloc, of Arnold Lunn and Evelyn Waugh, Alfred Noyes, Christopher Dawson and Christopher Hollis, Martin D'Arcy and E. I. Watkin, to name just a few whose writing delighted us and stretched our thinking. It was a Church in which Graham Greene's *The Power and the Glory* broke up cosy assumptions of Catholic morality and heroism, even more forcefully than Mauriac and Bernanos had done. It was a Church of Catholic action, of Young Christian Workers and Young Christian Students. Then there was this new movement of creative young women, called 'The Grail', who wore cloaks of brilliant colours and took over the Albert Hall for productions of *Everyman* and *The Hound of Heaven* which made their choreographic mark on the theatre of the time. Produced by women, acted by women who used powerful group movement, the Grail spoke the Word to the world.

Conversion to the Roman Catholic Church of privilege seemed the order of the day, and many of us presumed that a reasonably intelligent non-Catholic presented with the right book and the right argument would tumble into the one true fold. Argument is an operative word here. It was a time of delighted argument, and part of the joy of belonging to that Church of privilege was to have known Frank Sheed and Maisie Ward, the Catholic Evidence Guild, Father McNabb, the Ditchling Community and Eric Gill . . . I am amazed, even as I recall this litany of vitality, just how alive and full of certainties the Church of the 1930s was.

We were unaware of the strength of the right wing bias of the Catholicism of the time, and in this too, the Society of the Sacred Heart was a reflection of the Church's conservatism. Founded against the background of the French Revolution, the Society inevitably identified itself during the nineteenth century with 'reaction' and fostered the beleaguered city mentality of the Catholicism of that long-continued period. The expulsion of the religious orders and congregations from France in 1904, the deliberate choice of the Society to leave Mexico under Calles in the 1920s, and the experiences of religious during the Spanish Civil War, heightened the dramatic sense of confrontation of Church versus secular state. Communism, not Fascism, was the great enemy, and our Roman Catholic brothers did not go off to Spain to join the International Brigade.

But no one could have lived in the 1930s and been unmoved by unemployment and poverty, even if personally protected from their dehumanizing effects. At school we were brought up on the encyclicals of social justice, but it was all a bit theoretical and therefore unsatisfying and far away. A book of the period, *I Lived in a Slum* by Mrs Cecil Chesterton, was given me to read by one of the nuns and I remember daydreaming of ways by which I could mobilize public opinion against the evils about which she wrote. But whether, if war had not intervened, I should ever have done anything other than day-dream is a matter of doubt.

So the Society of the Sacred Heart in England reflected the Church of privilege and I belonged to that Church. Therefore my contemporaries and I, feeling at home in it, and proud of it, did not see ourselves as snobbish or arrogant. Elitist yes, because we believed that to belong to an élite was to be looked upon as a call to assume the role of responsibility for which our education had prepared us. In the war years when we broke through our various class barriers and met a different world on equal terms, we had no cause to be arrogant. In a short but educative time among the East-Enders of London returned from evacuation, I self-consciously tried to camouflage my accent and background. 'For gawdssike be yerself', a far, far better woman than I told me. From then on I was, and learnt much that my education had failed to teach me, amongst other things that the privileged did not have the monopoly of leadership.

How, from inside, did the Society of the Sacred Heart differ from my expectations of it? It looked and felt far more socially outdated than it had from the outside. The reason lay in the time gap that strict enclosure created in the thinking of those in authority, and that they in their turn prolonged at the level of imposed attitude. The most glaring effect of this was in the manner in which the categorization into choir religious and co-adjutrix sisters had come to be a sacred 'upstairs – downstairs' situation reminiscent of a Victorian great house. It was a division that had in no way shocked us in our school days. There we had loved the sisters far more freely than we had the mothers who relentlessly hounded our idleness. The sisters were our friends and an example of what the hiddenness of religious life was all about. They spoke to us of faith without preaching or teaching, and made promises of prayer for our intentions that we knew they would honour. Once my head-mistress said, looking at a Maltese sister refectorian: 'Have you ever thought what leaving home and family and sunshine must be for her? Think of the new generation of nieces and nephews she may never see.' We did think and we loved her, if it were possible, even more than before.

From the outside the two categories seemed more or less satisfactorily explained in Mother Janet Stuart's sketch of the Society of the Sacred Heart, when she answered the question asked even at the turn of the century and against a much more accepted situation of social differentiation: 'Why make two grades in the order?'

She wrote:

> If none could be received except in the grade of choir religious, many would have to be refused admission who are now in great honour and render untold service to the Society.
>
> . . . it would close the door against some precious vocations, rich with graces, and bringing a great dowry of virtues, whose *mark* replaces their signature in the Register of Vows. These marks are looked on with veneration, and those who use them have almost a distinction of their own, a flavour or originality in their words, an insight into spiritual things, a shrewd sense of many practical aspects of duty which gives them a value apart. They have not been filed down into uniformity by school books and exercises. They will become more and more rare.[6]

It was already past the period which the sentence 'they will become more and more rare' foretold. In 1943, there was no co-adjutrix sister in any of the communities in England without elementary education. Some had had secondary education or were trained teachers, even former students of our own teacher-training colleges. The Society, rightly valuing the faith dimension of this way of life, told of those choir nuns who had asked to enter as sisters and had been refused. This was hagiography, but it would have been more credible in the mid-twentieth century if the abnegation of those who accepted or chose the way of life of the co-adjutrix sister had been recognized for the act of faith it was.

The exclusiveness that shocked me after I entered spilled over into attitudes towards much that was not 'us' and 'ours'. There seemed to be a devastating certainty that whatever happened outside, whether it was a pattern of community living or the exploration of a new understanding of school organization, we of the Society already did it, or did it better, or did not do it because it was not worth doing. Enclosure seemed to have brought the rumbling waggon-train of the

---

[6] Janet Erskine Stuart, *The Society of the Sacred heart* (Roehampton Press 1914), p.26.

Society in England to a halt where self-questioning was concerned, and the ascendancy of the boarding school as the most important of the educational works seemed to prevent a free flow of ideas from the training colleges or maintained schools of the time, which were more in touch with the real world of the day.

But for the idealistic newcomer there were other important inside impressions. There was the complexity of human relationships and attitudes and the variety of personalities within the community which could be described as Dryden described Chaucer's *Canterbury Tales*: 'Here is God's plenty.' Together with those vocally influential few who talked with such an absurd lack of awareness of social and educational developments, were those actively influential many who had pioneered an Association of Convent Schools and hosted its pre-war meetings, opening new dimensions of interchange between the congregations of women. Someone at school at the time when I was a novice said her impression of the community was one of great vitality. Mine was of many giftedness: the artist, the musician, the thinker, the dreamer and the saint were all present but less audible than the snob. Faith was the dimension they lived, but together with that faith, there was an almost Edwardian worldliness which coloured attitudes and judgements.

'Worldliness' is a quaint old-fashioned word. It is the antithesis of the Gospel, and time has shown me that it has many more ways of manifesting its presence than through the exclusiveness of a particular social class. It will always be present where two or three are gathered together, even when they are gathered in Christ's name. The Zebedee family expressed one aspect, and it rears its head in today's egalitarianism under many different disguises.

I was a prig and I was shocked by some out-dated attitudes, but I was also forced to my knees in admiration at personal humble holiness and generosity. The living out of the Christian community must always be like that. Mother Stuart's 'little book of the sea' was as true a character sketch of the Society as Luke's idealized picture of the community of Jerusalem described in the Acts. Balance must be found in knowing that, like the institutional church which we women religious reflect, we are at the same time part of the sinful existential present, struggling to become what we are called to be and already the 'saints' of whatever community Paul scolds and praises in the immediacy of his letters.

So in the Society of the Sacred Heart idealism met reality and humanity. My father had brought me, not to the pious hymn singing of a church service, but to a circus. There was however a dimension missing in that circus of my new life. I had to come to terms with a world which lacked the friendship of men. I end therefore with one last moment of remembrance of what the Society of the Sacred Heart looked like from the inside: I was standing in my place in the community refectory as a novice, eyes downcast, and an expression of deceptive virtue pinned to my face. Inwardly I was savagely saying, 'Women, women, women . . .' Then I opened my eyes and looked at each nun, and, with enormous gratitude and joy said – 'WOMEN'.

5. Noviciate

Something of the externals of noviceship life has already been described. They were of minimal importance in comparison with what I saw to be the call to lay down my life for the brethren. I had understood that the price to be paid for this was celibacy accepted for the sake of the kingdom. The setting was irrelevant to the heart of my response to what this call was all about. Prayer, guidance in how to listen to the Spirit, the discipline of a common life, time to read and think and share with others what was the leading of God, and a sense of shared purpose were meaningful but the noviciate obstacle-race, with its ridiculous shibboleths, was not. I am by nature a conformist, and I can adapt myself to almost any situation if I find in it the approval of those I value. I was therefore perfectly ready to fit into the pattern, learn not only the steps of the expected dance, but even how to dance reasonably well. I have no doubt that God, who is so much greater than the little dances we invent in the hopes of pleasing him, accepted this situation of noviceship 'training' to deepen relationship with him. But when I hear those who went through the training canonizing its externals, I beg to disagree. Above all, I am amazed that those who canonize them wonder what the young who enter a religious congregation today have to give up. The answer is that they probably feel that they give up life itself, without any supposition that the promised hundred-fold will follow. Now, as then, the only reason for this is the folly of loving, the only way to live it is by loving more, and the only fruit, probably unfelt, is greater love. The external discipline of a noviciate must be geared to free the heart for this. It has no other purpose.

Obviously this was historically just what the external discipline was meant to be all about, some of the customs and attitudes going back to the desert fathers. We were introduced to their wisdom through the mediation of a seventeenth-century Jesuit classic, the writings of a certain Father Rodriguez, their tediousness mitigated by some excellent stories of what Cassian did, or did not say to the Abbot Moses, or Abba, or Elias. There was, too, the satisfaction of knowing that only the love of God would induce one to wear a night cap or leap out of bed well before dawn on a winter's morning. My sorrow is that although much of the life was neither good nor bad, merely peculiar, too much energy was wasted on conformity to its minutiae, and too much creativity on the need to walk a traditional tightrope acceptable to the elders of the congregation. I am not only thinking of the novices, but of those asked to direct them. For us at the receiving end, most of it was either dotty or funny – the doing of it – the failure to do it – the scoldings and 'penances' – all made for a bond of laughter and friendship, and tears, and a shared way of faith. But was it really worth the fuss? There were also those who were unable to laugh, who took the whole thing with a terrible seriousness. For them it proved damaging. Lives could be scarred and maturity impeded by over-concentration, not on the music or the rhythm of the dance, but on its toe-pointing demands.

The small group who were with me between May 1943 and December 1945 were in fact subjected to an interesting double-vision noviceship, as we changed Novice Mistresses in October 1944, sixteen months after I entered. Both Novice Mistresses were women of God, and it was good to have had this double vision. But the reason behind the change is a reflection, not only of the thinking of the Society, but of the understanding of religious life of the time. The manner of it has also given me an insight into the fears behind much that has been done in the institutional Church, and perhaps of the way that heresies are forced into being.

When I entered, the noviciate had been recently moved from a place of 'safety' in Scotland to become part, once again, of the community of the Roehampton boarding school, evacuated to a stately home. In the monastic tradition, the novices were not, in fact, part of the community but formed a separate community under the direction of the Novice Mistress. In the Society of the Sacred Heart this post was considered so important that the Mistress of Novices was not only appointed by the Mother General in Rome, but was also directly accountable to her. The English Vicariate, at that time, consisted not only of the English convents, but of a whole scattering of evacuated groups of nuns, children and students and of two convents in two countries united under a Superior Vicar: Malta had been part of the English Vicariate for a considerable number of years, and a university college in Bombay had been founded just before the outbreak of war. The Superior Vicar, Reverend Mother Archer-Shee, as local Superior of the community of the 'vicariate house', was obliged to keep in personal contact with each individual religious as well as with the houses of her Vicariate. It was important that she and the Mistress of Novices should understand each other and be in constant communication and it was in order that this might be ensured that the return of the novices from Scotland had been arranged. The uniformity which religious life tended to mistake for union had been badly shaken by the war situation, by the bombing of two of the London convents, and by the mitigation of the rules of enclosure during evacuation. There was also growing anxiety on the part of the Vicar at what the novices were reported to be learning from a woman of vision who did not quite fit the uniform mould.

Mother Shepherd, the Mistress of Novices, was a convert to Catholicism. Her education had been at the Glasgow High School during the distinguished headship of Dame Janet Spens, who remained a life-long friend. From there she had gone to Somerville to read English but ill health had prevented her from taking her degree. She had then tried her vocation as a Poor Clare, and had kept a love and admiration for the Franciscan ideal as she had seen it lived in the monastery during the few weeks of her postulantship before ill health again caused her to give up. Some time after leaving the Poor Clares she entered the Society of the Sacred Heart where she found a way of living her call fully and freely as a contemplative, and saw in the 'mixed life' a Gospel reality in tune with the twentieth century. As a young nun she had been a successful teacher in the school at Roehampton. After her profession she was for some time in charge of the organization of the curriculum, not only of the school, but, at a supervisory level, of the other schools of the Vicariate. She was named Mistress of Novices a few months before the outbreak of war, in recognition of her remarkable spiritual gifts, her power and vision as an educator and her great gentleness, integrity and charm as a person. She had clearly made an impression on the Mother General and the Assistants General during the statutory period of five months' preparation for final profession when she had been at the Mother House in Rome. She felt later that if her vision were suspect in the English Vicariate it was, in fact, in line with that of the wider congregation. Her naming as Mistress of Novices must, however, have been at the suggestion of the Superior Vicar, who, although she did not understand her, loved and admired her. But she presented an intolerable threat to a sacred *status quo*; her failure to fit the uniform mould, and disquiet at her methods of forming novices grew, because she looked critically at the religious life scene. In the Church of the day, in the religious life of the day and certainly in the Society of the Sacred Heart of the day, criticism was unacceptable. She loved the Society, and believed in its contemplative vision. She was aware, however, of the lack of true theological understanding of what was meant by contemplation, and she was concerned that the prayer-life of women religious be given a thorough theological and scriptural foundation.

Today it is impossible to remember areas of yesterday's fears. How could a religious congregation as international, intelligent and prayer-based as the Society of the Sacred Heart, have been so harnessed to its past that authority could only ratify as 'safe' for the 1940s, what was acceptable to the training of young religious of a century earlier?

At the centre of the fear was a nineteenth-century anxiety lest young women have ideas above their station, whatever that station might be. Whether socially, intellectually or spiritually, the young and not so young must be kept constantly aware of the rules of the game set out by tradition. It was a game in which the umpire's word was indeed final, and sometimes, at least for novices, required subservience of mind, even in methods of prayer. These were methods on which every religious in the society had been brought up and there were devotional books to aid meditation which were time-honoured. Mother Shepherd did not feel herself obliged to impose such uniformity on her novices, and rumour that she did not, spread panic in the ranks of the professed religious who felt it was their duty to report such deviations to the

unfortunate Superior Vicar. Worse still, novices were known
to be reading the great Teresa and John of the Cross, works
only hesitantly given as reading matter to older members of
the community. Probably more tiresomely, because of an
implied intellectual one-up-manship, novices were also going
about talking of their study of Aquinas as they devoured the
works of the various Thomistic theologians of the period. It
is easy to seem to ridicule this situation. It has too many
painful hierarchical parallels. There are no winners or losers
in the story, and no easy alternative to how things could have
been. Mother Shepherd said once that it is always the good
who cause most pain to the good. The experience of being
witnesses to the misunderstanding of the good by the good
was a very sad, but very formative one.

The root of misunderstanding is often in the definition of
terms, and the heart of this misunderstanding was the word
'contemplation'. I was present once when Mother Shepherd
and the foundress of the Grail, Baroness Yvonne Bosch, were
sharing ideas. Both agreed that there was no such thing as
an 'active' religious life. For both, the call to be a contemplative was synonymous with the call to a close following of
Christ and implicit through baptism in the call to be Christian. The popular tradition amongst the professed of the
Society of the Sacred Heart at that period saw 'contemplative'
prayer as an extraordinary grace, neither to be sought nor
prayed for. With this in mind Authority rightly feared the
'pretentiousness of a proud age' which made theological
reading and the study of the great mystics by young religious
something contrary to the humility of heart which they badly
needed to acquire. Mother Shepherd was convinced that most
of those who entered had already begun a journey of prayer
which was in some degree 'contemplative'. This she saw as
a flowering of the life of grace according to Thomistic tradition
and no more extraordinary than the faith, hope and charity
by which the Christian lived Christ. It was the ordinariness
of this way of 'wisdom', the *sapida scientia* of the gifts of the
Holy Spirit, that she stressed. Though the horizon was limitless she felt it important that we should be encouraged to
look towards it. From this came permission to read exten-
sively, and help in learning to listen to the Word in Scripture.
Each novice's prayer was considered to be individual and was
individually guided, and the only test of its rightness was a

growth in charity. Nothing, in fact, could have been nearer to the mind of St Madeleine Sophie or to the persons of the greatest influence in the society's history.

The foundress' humility of heart, power of patient waiting on the Spirit and 'simplicity of soul that seeks and longs for nothing but her God',[1] were based on philosophical and theological training exceptional in her day. She opened the way of deep prayer to those who thirsted for it, even as she led those who made it an end rather than a means to recognize their immaturity. Her successor as Superior General, in the mid-nineteenth century, was a convinced Thomist before Thomism was reinstated as the touchstone of sound seminary theological training. So no one in a congregation where philosophy was held dear as a basis for education should have taken exception to the ideas behind Mother Shepherd's training of her novices. But the fears grew. The novices exaggerated what had been taught them, and the young religious emerging from the noviciate tended to use the word 'contemplation' as a sort of party-banner under which they grouped themselves into a defensive band. Criticism of them spilled over into criticism of Mother Shepherd and made the novice and ex-novice freemasonry close ranks. This in turn isolated Mother Shepherd from her own peer-group who were the counsellors and wise women among the older professed, and with whom she should have been able to talk out her aims and methods. Many of them, because of a lack of real communication, were bewildered in finding an 'authority figure', a Novice Mistress, a councillor, looking to the future rather than simply to tradition for ratification of what she did.

So there was a crisis of loyalty at many levels, and the word 'loyalty' when it is used by the nice and the good is a frightening one unless it has loyalty to an ultimate truth as its starting place. I found myself remembering the pain and misunderstanding of the good by the good in my first year as a novice during the breakdown in communication and the witch-hunting which surrounded Corpus Christi, the short-lived catechetical college founded in the years immediately after Vatican II. I know that those of us who had the good fortune to have been, even for a short time, novices under Mother Shepherd, felt as did those who had been taught by

[1] Summary of Rule XIX, p.45.

Hubert Richards, that our eyes had been opened to new worlds and that nothing could make us unlearn what had been shown us. Our faith and our prayer had grown into an exultant conviction that God was God, that we were heirs to a great kingdom, and that the words of Leo the Great, 'O Christian, know thy dignity,' were addressed to each one of us. It was astonishing to us that authority could find fault with this, but communication was lacking and without it there can be no growth in understanding.

What has remained with me and grown in me since those short months of formation has been the joy that there is a limitless knowledge of the heart that far surpasses, but need never contradict or be separated from, knowledge of the mind. Mother Shepherd always used the Pauline phrase 'to have the mind of Christ' as the best description of our calling to union and conformity to the Heart of Jesus, and she helped me discover St Paul and, through him and Aquinas, the Church's teaching on grace and the indwelling of the Trinity. At the same time I rejoiced to know that a way of prayer that 'attends lovingly on God without any desire to feel or see further than to be in the hands of Him who now communicates himself . . . as the light of the sun to one whose eyes are open',[2] was simply the deepening of the way opened to me by my profoundly contemplative headmistress. This, we thought, was what our discipleship was all about, and our post-noviceship lives as educators would be to lead others in their turn to know their dignity as co-heirs of Christ. We were convinced of the truth of Irenaeus, 'The glory of God is man fully alive', a quotation not so often used in those days; we were taught to complete it, 'and the life of man is the contemplation of God'. Unlike our critics, assailed by fears, we were assured that contemplation was life, not removal from it.

Mother Shepherd often spoke of our educational mission in terms of the Dominican call, '*contemplata aliis tradere . . .*', to pass on to others what we have seen in prayer. This is a truth affirmed in everything we say about our mission and our formation for it today. In the climate of 1944, quoting a Dominican axiom would have been immediately suspect.

Sometimes Mother Shepherd dreamed about the future and would share her idea of a way of religious life which seemed

2   *Ascent of Mt Carmel*, Book II, Ch. 15.2.

to her might one day come to be. I do not think that she saw
the Society taking this shape, merely that it was a shape which
she felt fulfilled the demands of a contemplative/apostolic life
and fitted the pattern of the world of today and tomorrow.
Her name for this 'order' was Aedes Christi, the House of
Christ. Each community of the order would be a 'house of
Christ', a place of quiet and prayer and 'indwelling' open to
whomsoever would wish to come and share with the
community the riches and insights of their life. She always
envied the monastic hospitality of the Benedictines, where
men were welcomed by the community in their refectory and
to their office, and felt that the over-enclosure of women's
orders was out of place in the twentieth century. She thought
that the communal prayer of this dream-community should
be open for all to join in and learn to love. Above all, she
saw each house as a place where counsel, friendship and
direction in prayer would be available. These were the bare
bones of the dream, and I have been reminded of it time and
again since the post-Vatican-II renewal of religious life, and
the experimentation with new forms of urban monasticism,
as well as our own post-enclosure understanding of
community and community mission. One of the points that
belonged to her dream and which reflected her own thinking
on formation was that this new 'order' would have no rule of
silence. She taught that silence had to come from the desire
to be still, just as 'recollection' (that tiresome imposition of
lowered eyes, hands folded at the waist and measured step)
must reflect an inner integration or be mere posturing.

How would Mother Shepherd have approached formation
today? Would she have approved of the ways by which
contemplative life is treated as a 'must' and the word not
banned but sometimes too facilely bandied about? Like many
who were ahead of their time, she might well have proved a
conservative in the face of the open flood-gates. We shall
never know as she died in the spring of 1947.

Meanwhile in the autumn of 1944 this strange, disturbing,
challenging and unconventional noviceship ended. The
Superior Vicar seized an opportunity to visit war-battered
Malta, getting herself there in an RAF bomber, and thereby
disappearing into the unknown for an unpredictable period
of time. In fact she managed to go from Malta to Italy, and
eventually reached Rome and the Mother House by various

means of Army transport. When she returned it was not only with an account of this remarkable journey and of the state of the communities in Malta and southern Italy, but with the mandate from the centre of the Society to replace Mother Shepherd by Mother Bennett as Mistress of Novices. Mother Shepherd was to be sent as Superior to the community in Oxford, the Society's house of studies. Mother Bennett, called to reform us, would be asked to leave responsibility as Superior of a number of scattered evacuated communities in the north and the organization of the return to the Newcastle campus of two maintained schools, a Direct Grant grammar school and a teacher training college. In exchange she would take on three novices and three postulants.

Mother Shepherd had two important teaching quotations: the first, that growth in charity was the only valid test whether what was being done, followed, promulgated, was of God or not. To this she always added that charity needs to be of the mind as much as of the heart, for to follow the truth in love the truth must be discerned and perceived. The merely emotional, sometimes mistaken for the heart, can block it. Those of course were the days when we were told that 'feelings do not count', but although I have come to realize how much they do count, this testing of the good spirit or the bad is Ignatian and sound. Where there is no true charity in the head and heart there can be no peace, no place for Christ. Needless to say, we as noviciate failed that test with flying colours as we faced this moment of 'obedience'. The second teaching quotation was from the Pseudo-Dionysius' *Treatise on the Divine Names*: Hiorethius was seen to be 'perfect' because he not only learnt, 'but suffered Divine things'. '*Non solum discens sed patiens divina*'. We were certainly not 'patient of' the Divine in this, but we learnt and suffered divine things through it, and in the end we grew. That, after all, is what formation is really about.

It was a traumatic testing however; and if, as novices, we lacked faith and charity, the faith and charity that sustained both the sacker and the sacked through this clear vote-of-no-confidence situation was admirable. In fact, the faith and charity that sustained Mother Bennett was heroic. It would have been hard to find two people more dissimilar; Mother Shepherd was tall, gentle, slightly stooping, scholarly, with brown eyes and a habit of saying 'bless her' or 'bless him'

after anything that might have seemed to border on the judgemental, however well deserved. Her most uncharitable, as
opposed to intelligently critical, remark was once when a
large number of sheep and lambs surrounding the stable
chapel were in full spring voice. She was then heard to
murmur thoughtfully that they made her think of mint sauce.

Mother Bennett was tiny, blue-eyed, dynamic, forthright,
practical, impatient, with the simplicity of a child and the
courage of a lion. She was clearly bored stiff by novices.
However she set about the task of reformation with vigour
and humour. We were put on a diet of the traditional meditation books, and were expected to read out our points for
the next morning's meditation after night prayers. When we
rebelled, which we did explosively and without inhibition,
she was provoked into saying, 'If I can obey, you can obey,'
which gave us a clear indication that the system of reformation was received rather than initiated.

What was the value of this double-vision noviciate and
what was its relevance to the whole process of evolution in
religious life? I think that perhaps it was the earthing of the
prophetic and visionary in a practical present which religious
need at every stage. I look back with regret at the way in
which reformation and revolt were obliged to make issues
where no issues need have been. The word 'wisdom' was
almost banished from our vocabulary, and when my closest
friend and fellow-rebel once started talking about the
indwelling of the Trinity, she was told firmly that she was
learning to be a religious of the Sacred Heart not a daughter
of the Trinity or sister of the Holy Ghost. 'It's all one to me,
Mother,' was her reply in the true submissive spirit of our
fellowship which never ceded the last word to another, least
of all to newly imposed authority.

When I think of Mother Bennett, the unwilling agent of
reform, it is in a blue working apron with her overskirt tucked
up, carrying a saw or rake, and laughing. There might be
rebellion and clashes of personality but sanity and laughter
are in the end irresistible, and she brought us a great deal of
both. Obedience was her own personal sheet-anchor, and it
was over the question of obedience that there was the most
serious problem of authority versus Mother Shepherd, or
rather of two authorities acting in the same sphere. With a
different understanding of obedience there would have been

no confusion, and there was no failure of obedience on the part of Mother Shepherd or of her understanding that true obedience is never blind. There was confusion, greatly increased by the group antagonism that met some of the young religious who had gone into the communities from the noviciate.

It was a relief to feel under the reforming new leadership that the intangible barriers of suspicion with which the noviciate had been surrounded were down. It was good that Mother Bennett brought us, as novices, air from the world of that other Church some of us had never known. Before becoming Superior she had been headmistress of the grammar school at Newcastle during the hard years of the 1930s and she loved and was loved by everyone connected with it and with the wider community of the area. When war broke out and she was named Superior of the large community at the centre of the campus and all its flourishing works, she had to take responsibility for the dispersal of the nuns and the setting up of communities in various places of evacuation. All this meant adaptation to circumstances, the lifting of the rules of enclosure and a life much closer to the ordinary than had been possible for pre-war Sacred Heart nuns. Something of this was happening in our evacuated boarding school and in the noviciate itself, but the northern scene foreshadowed more closely the religious life of the future. For Mother Bennett herself the experience necessarily exploded reliance on any sacrilized *status quo* and made the nonsense of novices who dramatized the petty look as ridiculous as, in fact, it was. She never had to walk the tightrope balancing her free and real-istic methods against the fears of the elders. Her own life of unself-regarding tough service gave her unassailable credibility and her immense simplicity never needed to question the straightforward line of conduct presented by duty. She was good for us, perhaps most of all in her breezy dismissal of us which put into proportion so much heightened over-awareness bred by noviciate isolation. Because she herself hated isolation, we were as quickly involved in the school as canon law allowed, and this opened our hot-house life to the air.

So noviceship, discipleship, the time of being in a special way a learner, pointed towards much that would come later. We were out of the traditional setting. We had been challenged by some critical thinking and our minds and hearts opened to the wide horizons of God. We were aware of an authority, in the person of the Superior Vicar, for whom the *status quo* was sacred, and who yet was a person of sensitivity and courage and faith. We had been under the direct guidance of a Mistress of Novices who did not fit the accepted mould, and of one who, without in any way being restricted by it, did. We as novices therefore came under the influence of three great women, one who looked to the future, and paid for it dearly, one who looked to the past and was crushed by the present, and one who dealt with the present in unquestioning faith and who lived to lead us all, when she became Superior Vicar, into the future. We had also seen the pain which each could cause the other and, with shame, the pain our own tangled loyalties could inflict.

6. Signs and Symbols

A few months before I made my first vows I suddenly knew that the only wasted time in life is the time spent in not loving. And that seemed to me then, and seems to me now, is what the vows of religion are all about: they are a public declaration that one has committed oneself to this loving 'even unto death', in and through and with Jesus, by the power of the Holy Spirit to the glory of God the Father. Like Mary, the vowed life –

> This one work has to do –
> Let all God's glory through . . .[1]

The paraphernalia of religious life seemed a heavy superstructure to build round this Christ-evident way of responding to the Gospel. But there is something important in the public dimension of the act, and in the visibility of the life, and for my generation both were present in a way I would only have questioned in moments of fleeting illumination.

Today, the prophetic value of the vows is perhaps more stressed than the legal. But vows if they are made publicly must have the clarity of legal content, and this is as necessary today as it was yesterday. There is less emphasis, however, on what constitutes breaking a vow, and less emphasis on the value of final profession weighed, for example, in hypothetical scales against the value of martyrdom. As I remember this particular bit of Thomistic speculation, and my joy in its significance, I am also reminded sharply of the measurement orientation of all our religious thinking at that not too distant time. The classroom questions of – 'Is it a sin if . . .?' 'How far can you go . . .?' 'What do seven years and seven quaran-

---

[1] G. M. Hopkins, 'The Blessed Virgin Mary Compared to the Air We Breathe'.

tines mean for the souls in purgatory?' had their counterpart in the adult world of total commitment in both marriage and religious life.

When we left the noviceship we made perpetual conditional vows that bound us to the Society of the Sacred Heart but did not bind the Society to us. That is to say we had the security of knowing that they were vows 'for life' and that the Society would never now ask us to leave except for grave reasons. Authority in the Society however reserved the right to refuse final profession if, for example, during the years before we were eligible, it was seen that we were unhappy and therefore unsuited to its way of life. The thought that this might happen to me never crossed my mind, and my first vows were as absolute for me as was my final profession. In fact the 'Yes, Father, with all my heart' at the profession ceremony of August 1943 was my 'final profession' as far as I was concerned. The long eight years of being a learner still had to be completed however, before I could make my final commitment publicly and with the full acceptance of the Society.

At the time of final profession two vows of devotion were added to the three vows of poverty, chastity and obedience: a vow of stability, which bound us irrevocably to the Society, and a vow which consecrated us to the education of youth. We were taught that though these were vows of devotion they were by no means 'poor relations'. Because they were made to God they consecrated what was undertaken in a special way, but they did not of course constitute the state of religious life as did the three vows of religion.

The vow of stability to the Society had its roots in the importance given to the sign value of vows which was so strong in the Church of the nineteenth century. St Madeleine Sophie wished to obtain for the Society the right for its religious to be as 'bound' as the Church would allow. The solemn vows which were permitted by the Church only to the old monastic orders were the model for this binding.

Her desire was understandable in the turbulent period of post-revolutionary France when the whole fabric of established religious life had been destroyed. The resurgent orders and congregations and those newly founded give the impression of new life struggling into recognition through a tangled undergrowth of old dead wood, trying to make patterns of the past match the demands of a new France. The official Church of the period, meanwhile, performed canonical acrobatics to keep up with the bewildering number of religious groups seeking approbation from the Holy See.

St Madeleine Sophie's contemplative vision led her and her early companions and councillors to choose the way of approbation which would make religious of the Society as much 'nun' as it was possible to be, without the solemn vows of the monastic orders.

The price that had to be paid for this was an enclosure which became more and more out of keeping with the work undertaken. As late as 1952 the question of the suppression of enclosure was put forward with great insistence, for consideration by the highest authority of the Society in its General council. The reply was that 'Enclosure in the Society is directly dependent upon the vow of stability, as papal enclosure is to solemn vows'.[2]

The conclusion was, therefore, that enclosure was a serious matter since it was linked with the vow, and the vow of stability made the simple vows almost equivalent to solemn vows. The writings of the foundress on the matter show how much she saw the whole question as being an indication to those who were in contact with us that we put our life bound to union with the Heart of Christ before everything else no matter what the inconvenience, or in the case of family ties, the pain. So when time came for final profession in the Society, the canonical superstructure which ratified publicly our will to belong to God as absolutely as possible, was complex, but it looked to the end which we wanted.

I have lived to see dispensation from final vows sought and granted with an ease that was unthinkable less than twenty years ago. I have myself encouraged professed religious to ask for such dispensation, but the end which St Madeleine Sophie wanted for the religious of the society is the end we all want, individually and as a body, and that is the absolute living of love, bound to a God who is love, through the Heart of Jesus.

We all want final profession to be for ever, and we know that the fidelity of God is not in question in this covenant. But we have a very different idea today of the efficacy of the outward to create an inward change of heart, and a less

[2] Jeanne de Charry XXIV General Cong. cit.

idealized conviction that what we have done is necessarily objectively the best. I am also well aware of the difficulty of searching in spirit and in truth for the most honest and Christ-centred choice of action. For that reason, I cannot find myself always at peace at decisions taken to retract solemn promises.

Religious profession and marriage have so much in common, and never have the two had such reason to compare experience as they have today. Frère Max Thurian of Taizé in his book, *Marriage and Celibacy*, made the pertinent comment that Christian marriage and Christian celibacy are both impossible to human nature. But both call for the declaration by men and women that, with the grace of God, human loving can be for ever and can be faithful in the face of great hardship. In Christian marriage and in vowed celibacy the response to a call to lay down one's life is the heart of the matter, because it is at the heart of being Christian, but it must be done freely for love. In order to love truly and in order to lay down one's life for love, a level of maturity of which perhaps we were insufficiently aware in the past, is needed. The need is the greater today where social structures supportive of choice hardly exist, and the period of adolescence, or self-discovery without responsibility, is prolonged.

By adding the vow of stability, which led to an enclosure increasingly out of keeping with the work of education, it is questionable whether any religious of the Sacred Heart remained more faithful to the vows of religion. Few professed left the congregation before Vatican II, and those who did went with a sense of failure and alienation. But this was in line with the low rate of divorce among contemporary Catholics, while 'defection' from the priesthood was rare.

Enclosure is the key to much that divides the past from the present, and the past of the Society divided it from the local Church. Once enclosure was lifted, adaptation to a way of life out of line with our history was not merely shocking to those who over-idealized us, but symbolized the revolution taking place at a far deeper level of theology. From within our communities the abrogation of enclosure after Vatican II was something to which we very happily accustomed ourselves. But whether or not, after nearly twenty years, we have yet really moved out of our mental enclosure is questionable. For this reason it is worth while examining the two symbols of what we were. They are at one level superficial, but at another deeply significant: they are enclosure and habit. They are closely linked.

Enclosure meant in effect that every house of the society was a self-sufficient community cut off from the world outside. Within the house a part was reserved for the nuns only. As religious we left the house and grounds only to move from one convent to another. By the 1930s and increasingly after the war, we were allowed to go out to hospitals for treatment, preferably those run by religious, and to some educational meetings and courses. The purpose of it all, not unlike that of those who fled to the desert in the early days of Christendom, was to create a 'city of God' freed from the pressures of 'the world' where a climate of prayer, quietness, order and charity favoured an 'other worldly' life. The rules of perspective in drawing are a good analogy for the focus of life in an enclosed convent. Every line in a drawing leads to a vanishing point, the focus of the picture. The focus in the convent was the direction towards which each religious looked, and the whole way of life was arranged to facilitate the looking, the contemplation of an unseen world.

The strict timetable for the nuns and for the school, the bells, the silence, the forms of recreation, office, prayer, work in common and different areas of strictly subordinated responsibility all contributed to a 'beauty of order'. In a monastic setting this was to free the mind to pray always, and in the 'mixed life' to which we were committed, that was the hope of those who walked through the doors of the enclosure from a heavy day in the school.

As a young nun I did not question the value of enclosure, and would have argued as well as anyone in its defence as an insurance of the primary call to the contemplative life. But I had reason to be embarrassed at the way in which it was interpreted several times in the ten years before Vatican II, when I was headmistress of a boarding school at Tunbridge Wells. We were in close touch with the parish and, on the whole, liked by an admirable team of priests who were at the same time often understandably irritated by our peculiar restrictiveness.

On one occasion the parish priest, a very real friend, asked if we would allow the Brownies to use our hockey field as a place to have their picnic. They had been molested on the local common by a man who was going about exposing

himself, and the Brown Owl, a pillar of the Church, felt that
they would be safe within our grounds. I presumed the answer
could only be yes, but had no authority to say so without
asking my superior. To my stupefaction she said, 'No'. She
was a woman of wide experience and warm heart, someone
who was personally critical of the snobbery of the Society as
she had met it in her younger days, someone free in herself
and capable of freeing others. But she saw this use of the
grounds as an encroachment on the rule of enclosure, and felt
she had no right to make exceptions without betraying her
trust as superior to uphold the rule. I had the task of saying
'No' to the parish priest, without going into the details of
why. And what would have been the point? They would have
made the inexplicable execrable. But I remember going into
the garden after my shame-filled encounter and weeping with
rage and frustration and total disbelief that such a reply to
such a request had anything to do with what our lives were
about. There could be other examples. I have used this one
to show how a form of unrecognized idolatry alien to the
whole spirit of St Madeleine Sophie had crept into our religious life.

Means so easily become ends. Enclosure for us was the
price exacted by a nineteenth-century Church for the right to
make vows as binding as possible. Prayer, which these vows
safeguarded, tended in its turn to become an idolatry, because
it was equated by some with unchangeable measurements of
time, a 'something' to be accomplished almost as though it
were an end in itself. I had been put on my guard as a
schoolgirl by my already much-quoted headmistress, against
becoming a practising Catholic non-Christian. This was not
the only time I had to face the fact that I was trapped into
being a faithful religious non-Christian, and I suspect that
there are others of my generation who shared that experience.

Even as I cringe inwardly remembering this and like incid-
ents linked with enclosure, and see how far it removed us
from the life of the local Church, I also remember some of
the restrictions that made that local Church in its turn less
than Christian. Priests were made, by hierarchical authority,
to feel and act as I was made to feel and act, though for
them the enforced withdrawal was behind the barricades of
denomination. So once again I see women religious reflecting
the face of the institutional church. I realize that what was

reflected was not simply a mirror-image of the actions themselves, but of the power of authority motivated by fear. In
order to be a faithful link in a chain of command that reached
back into remote tradition, authority in the Church and in
religious life enforced actions that were certainly far removed
from the spirit of Christ.

After Vatican II enclosure ceased to exist for any religious
other than those under solemn vows, and for the national and
local Church the barricades between the denominations were
at least lowered, if not dismantled. Vows of devotion were no
longer encouraged. Religious dress for nuns was modernized
and simplified. We had, therefore, to face the loss of a badge
of identity which was more important for us as individuals
than the restrictions of enclosure which affected our corporate
life. For me the two are closely bound together, and it was
the experience of coming out of the citadel of enclosure that
made me see the habit, or religious dress, whatever that vague
term may mean, as a counter-sign of my commitment. The
habit, apparently so external and unimportant, not only was,
but still is, disproportionately significant.

When I received the habit and became a novice in 1943 I
was relieved to feel that at last I looked outwardly like the
nun I was trying to be. St Madeleine Sophie had insisted that
when the religious dress of the Society was adopted it should
be 'simple and common to all'. She did not want something
that recalled the monastic. Without the veil the choir nun's
habit, until 1967, was not unlike the basic dress of the Jane
Austen period. That of the co-adjutrix sisters was in many
ways more attractive and simple. The choir nun's 'pie frill'
bonnet which tended to collapse in the rain, was probably the
ordinary wear of the middle-class matron, while the sister's
ungoffered half-bonnet was closer to the peasant costume of
the early nineteenth century. However, by the mid-twentieth
century no one in their right mind could have called the habit
simple, and for anyone entering between 1914 and the late
1960s, a feeling of putting on fancy dress was both satisfying
(here at least was something to prove a different way of life)
and tiresome. The number of strings to be tied, petticoats to
be worn and underwear to be coped with was astonishing
and hilarious. But the result declared to all, 'I am a Sacred
Heart nun and proud of it,' and I remember both enjoying
and being liberated by that assurance.

When I was at Oxford as an undergraduate between 1947 and 1950 I was able to test out the symbol of the habit away from its convent setting. Linked with the complexities of our particular type of enclosure, it not only differentiated me from my fellow students but also from my fellow religious of other congregations. Non-Catholic friends who chaperoned me beyond the statutory five minutes allowed for lone walking outside enclosure, would sometimes wince when Roman Catholic cyclists shouted, 'Are you the Holy Child?' across the traffic jams of Carfax or St Ebbes. More so when they heard me shouting back, 'No, I'm the Sacred Heart'. As time went on, my height, my pie-frill bonnet and I, had our uses and 'Meet me by Mother Wilson' was apparently a good way of linking up with a friend in the crush of a Schools' lecture room. I certainly found the habit no barrier to friendship, and in a world where oddities have always been acceptable, it was often a good talking point to be recognizably a nun. What I was about was clearly academic, and my dress the symbol of a purposeful, disciplined, prayer-orientated community way of life which might have its apparently pointless rules, but was in tune with the university setting of the time. In fact Oxford and the Society of the Sacred Heart were both content to be out of tune with a swiftly changing world, and my experience of wearing religious dress outside enclosure during my student days was very different from my experience of wearing it twenty years later in an entirely secular setting.

When Vatican II called on women religious to modernize their habits, we of the Society of the Sacred Heart found ourselves catapulted into a particularly unbecoming nun's uniform. In 1967 hair was not yet on view; by 1969 it could be shown, and by 1971 the possibility of wearing 'secular' dress was open to those who wished to do so. It is a waste of time to recall the trauma of these changes inside and outside the cloister. They are the measure of the identification of the nun with an outdated symbol, and the agitation caused by our change in appearance is still symptomatic of the emotional resistance to any change in the Church we symbolize.

The citadel mentality of the Church had been challenged to accept the theology of a pilgrim people of God; the walls of enclosure safeguarding the contemplative life for apostolic religious had been removed; the place of the laity had been recognized; the total domination of the Church by clerics had been questioned. Sisters brought up to respect the Church's division into cleric and lay found that, like it or not, they were of the laity. Then as they looked into the meaning of the word 'secular' now being used as opposed to 'sacred', many found it good, expressing the Christian belief that the risen Jesus belongs to this time and this world. Many of us saw more clearly than ever before that the work of the Church we mirror is to be the good news that what is secular waits to be made holy by his presence, and that we Christians are that presence.

Given that belief, why should sisters be expected to dress up in a way that deliberately separates them from this world to which they belong and wish to belong? What is particularly holy in adopting the colour of mourning, or a uniform that declares that they belong to a caste apart? Why in this matter of colours, for example, should pink be shocking and blue respectable? The whole question would be ridiculous were it not so serious. It is serious because ecclesiastical officialdom unconsciously sees in the repudiation of uniform by women religious, a sign, not only of the independence of women, but of a whole perception of what the Church is. What has happened to nuns at dress and community level since Vatican II is an awe-inspiring model of the post-Vatican-II Church. In the countries of a conservative Church where there has been minimal outward refurbishing of the ecclesiastical structures, nuns are everywhere as veiled as Muslim wives, with perhaps a slight lifting of the hem line. In countries where the Church is pushing its frontiers and where the laity are accepting their responsibility, nuns are freed to use their energies for the kingdom, and are no longer conspicuous by a way of dress that cuts them off from their fellow Christians. In countries like Latin America where the hope of the Church is already seen to be in the community of the faithful, and nuns are an integral part of that community, the sign of their consecration is their manner of listening to the Word made flesh in the now of today. But, alas, nuns without habits are women and women are still for the bureaucratic Church a bad thing unless well under male control. That is the psychology of this situation.

For the theology of it I examine my own experience and admit that there are as many good apostolic reasons for wearing a religious habit as there are against wearing it. The reason why I find it unacceptable in modern religious life has nothing whatever to do with the 'good' that it may or may not achieve or the false image it may or may not project. It is rooted in an experience of Church and the conviction of a theology that can no longer accept a people of God divided into first- and second-class citizens.

Directly I found myself driving a car, shopping, travelling on public transport dressed up to appear holier than thou, I was uncomfortable. The discomfort was enhanced by those who liked seeing me defined as a nun. I found it touching but wrong that far older people should give up their places to me on a bus, or that conductors should refuse my fare. It was moving to know that the cloth was so valued, at least by some, but it was saying something about my way of life that was untrue.

The real questioning came for me between the autumn of 1970 and the spring of 1971, on two significant occasions. The first was when as Headmistress I took a party of sixth formers to the play *Abelard and Heloise*, based on Helen Waddell's incomparable novel. It was a play worth seeing for the talking points that it afforded. A year or two previously there would have been no question of my accompanying the group. I would then have used its message by hearing from the girls what they had seen and comparing it with the novel which I knew well. Should I still choose not to go at a time of habited unenclosure? As I thought about this I saw that my reason for not going would in no way be because of the castrated Abelard's anguished identification of his manhood with his genitalia. It would have been because my presence as a nun would have felt wrong, not for my sake, not for the sake of the sixth-form I was taking, but for the sake of the general audience in the theatre. I would have been out of place, a scandal to those who would have identified me with an apartness of holy virginity shockingly exposed to a play suitable for sixth-formers but not for the person entrusted with their education.

Here was one of those moments of illumination. If my job put me, as a nun, into situations where the sign of my being a nun was wrong, either the sign was no longer significant of what I really was and what I really did or I should not, as a nun, do the job I was doing. Did being a nun exclude me in public, not in private, from that which was right for lay colleagues and for girls of sixteen, seventeen and eighteen? What was I being protected from at least in the expectations of the non-nun world? Needless to say I went to the play, dressed up in a coat and skirt taken out of a cupboard labelled 'clothes for the poor', and with a false bun pinned on to the back of my head. Surrounded by fifty or so sixth-formers in the cheaper seats of the gallery I was feeling happily anonymous. Then a voice from several rows below rang out with joyful discovery: 'O Mother Wilson, what are you doing? I recognized your voice and could not think where it was coming from . . .' Every head was turned. Luckily the bun held bravely in its place.

A much deeper insight came in the spring of 1971. I was given the opportunity to make a retreat in the 'Maison Familiale' near Beauvais, run by Abbé Caffarel, an apostle of prayer as a way of life for all Christians. I understood that this was to be a silent retreat, but that Père Caffarel liked to gather a group of between thirty and thirty-five retreatants who were as representative as possible of the 'people of God'. Because of this he wished the religious or priests making it to be kept to a number approximately that of a cross-section of a local Church. He also wished his retreatants to discover their identity as a community of believers, and asked the religious to come in secular dress and the priests, except during the concelebration of the Eucharist, to be equally unidentifiable. This request was in itself the presentation of a point of view I found important, and I went off to France in the poor-cupboard coat and skirt and the now famous detachable bun, open to conversion in ways wider than those usual in my expectations of a retreat.

In this group of thirty-five we were three, or possibly four, nuns and two or three priests. Some of the others were young students, there was a farmer and his wife, freed to come because 'bonne-maman' had taken on the children, there was a First-World-War widow in her late seventies, a husband and wife belonging to a community of artists and writers, a comte or a marquis and his comtesse or marquise, a widow of the Second World War, a worker from a Paris factory, and others . . . These are faces and backgrounds that come to my mind as I remember the group. Indeed I do often remember them in my prayer of gratitude for the experience I received among them of being Church. Although we were in silence after the first evening meal until the last meal before departure, we were very conscious of becoming a community, bound to each other, aware of each other, and accepting each other.

My fullest realization of what this meant came one evening during the Eucharist. The 'Maison Familiale' was a nineteenth-century château and its chapel a converted room with seats encircling the altar. It was so close to the Vatican II liturgical reforms that it was the first time that I had heard Mass in French. The words of consecration, 'Ceci est mon corps . . .' struck home with powerful immediacy. I looked round the circle and knew that we were, each one of us, in the now of that moment in time, the Body of Christ. We were all trying to be true to our calling to leave all and follow Jesus in the way of celibacy or widowhood, or marriage, or priesthood, or religious life. It would have felt as unfitting, as absurd, for me and the other religious women present to have been dressed up to express our difference as it would for the widows to have been veiled in crêpe or the farmer to have worn a smock or the marquis the family coat of arms on a chain round his neck. We were who we were, the Body of Christ, and we needed each other to make that body whole. Only those amongst us who loved most truly were closer to God than the others, and only he knew who those were.

I was never again, after that experience, able to wear my World-War-II-V.A.D.-in mourning-church-uniform with any sense of integrity. If I were obliged to return to something of the sort today, I should feel myself unfaithful to the Gospel and unfaithful to what I believe the Church to be.

7. A Life Handed Over

Consideration of the two vows of devotion, that of stability and the vow to consecrate ourselves to the education of youth, led, in the last chapter, to an exploration of the effect of enclosure and of that other outward sign of apartness, the habit. These and the desire for a devotional multiplication of vows belong to the past. The essential consecration of religious life through the vows of religion, of obedience, poverty and chastity, remains the key to what makes monks, sisters, brothers and priests in the clerical orders what they are in the Church. Will this always be so? It is asked whether the making of these vows according to the 'evangelical counsels' is acceptable. Whether too, in the face of the devastations of real poverty it is not an insult to our starving brothers and sisters to take a vow under that name and then to sit down for the rest of our lives to an assured succession of adequate meals. Above all, why should obedience, poverty and chastity be seen to be something peculiar to religious? They are part of the evangelical life of every Christian, lived according to different callings, but all three a necessary sign of the one consecration, the one vocation, which continues Christ's incarnational presence till the end of time: baptism.

'I live now not with my own life but with the life of Christ who lives in me.'[1] This points to transforming union, that mystical identification with Christ through his Spirit which is our life as baptized members of his body. We shall be led to the fullness of that life by greater, more selfless loving. What we call heaven, our final fullness of life, will be knowing even as we are known, being like him because we shall see him as he is.

I once saw a crucifix with a hollow place at the heart of

[1] Galatians 2.20.

the crucified figure. It seemed to be a true symbol of the given-away self that is filled by the Other, and that even in the giving calls forth a self at last fulfilled and whole. The vows say stumblingly, blindly, that because God is God and I am I, that is the way I want my life to be, now, not later, and that everything that I choose in this life must be directed to that end.

The better we understand baptism, the better we understand the vows. The more we explore Christianity, the better we understand baptism. The fact is that Christianity is a relationship first and a religion only in so far as we need a clearly seen channel of encounter with the sought-for Christ and the tangible means by which we can express that encounter. The specifically religious element of being bound to God and to each other should intensify our awareness that to be a Christian is synonymous with being a mystic; therefore we should not need vows other than those of our baptism to be both Christian and mystic. But there is something in the personal encounter of the relationship to which baptism opens us which demands, for some, a public declaration of absolute and primal commitment. I return to Joyce Carey and the 'recognition of the heart', and to my own experience of freedom that could not be free in the face of an inescapable love. Marriage in the true Christian context is the commitment of each to the other so that the choice of God is made, and the seeking of his will is done, together. Celibate life in community expresses a singleness of purpose in a wider context of committed relationship. Both face the problem of an over-idealism which expects support from the other or others rather than recognition of the call to put love where there may sometimes seem to be no love, to build daily on what has gone before, and to make mutual forgiveness and acceptance the basis of a liturgy of life. Both need the assurance of having put into words what is in their hearts.

When I think of vows I am reminded of a caption under a nineteenth-century drawing of a Quaker wedding: '. . . No vows do our union enforce, But who ever heard of a Quaker divorce?' Presumably no one would be a Quaker for the purely social reasons for which many have been Christians since the Edict of Constantine made it a respectable way of life. No one would marry a fellow-Quaker without the Quaker commitment forming a bond deeper than that which unites many who go into conventional Christian marriage. Be that as it may, those who choose to bind themselves by marriage vows, choose to do so, not to ensure themselves against possible divorce, but because of the need of love to express itself as strongly and as publicly as possible. The audacity of saying 'unto death' for all to hear is an act of faith in the fidelity of God, who makes an eternal covenant with our vacillating, human half-loving. No vows need enforce this, but the clarification of intention in words has a power and a sign value that cannot be lightly foregone. However, as society changes, the content of the formulation used to express commitment will change. The words may be the same, but the expectation of their meaning differs. This is true of religious vows, and though I have not changed my desire to be bound unto death, I have changed in my understanding of how I live out the way in which the vows so bind me.

The changes that reflect the changed image of the Church are seen most clearly in the area of obedience; the changes that reflect the attitude of contemporary Christians to the world are in the area of poverty; and the changes which reflect a better understanding of the human psyche are in the area of chastity. But the three vows are facets of the one gift, and if the vows are to free the person vowed to love, they are also a way of integration which should make the person vowed more capable of the responsibility of being human, and therefore more capable of freeing others to love and of accepting their love in return.

The over-emphasis in the past on obedience to the Superior and obedience to the rule grew socially and ecclesiastically out of the hierarchical concept of life. This matched a desire for certainty on the part of the person wishing to make vows that he or she was 'truly seeking God', truly seeking to do his will, a will seen somewhat statically as a mapped-out path to be found and followed.

St Benedict has been blamed for the effects of references made in his rule to the Abbot as Christ. In fact Chapter II of the Rule of St Benedict says: 'We believe that in the monastery the abbot takes the place of Christ', a very much less absolute statement. In that remarkable legislation, who, in fact, is responsible for asking this monk among other monks, a brother among his brothers, to take on Christ-like leadership, except the body of the brethren? If after that the brethren turn whatever he suggests into a military command, they are misinterpreting both the Rule and the Gospel.

The centralized government of the post-Reformation Church and of non-monastic religious life was far more military in legislation for community than it was for the monastic. In many international congregations the pyramid was made up of all the communities, provinces and countries, and authority was often the more imposed and centralized as the congregation was widespread. As in many other nineteenth-century congregations of women, the pattern of authority in the Society of the Sacred Heart was modelled on that of the Society of Jesus, with a Superior General elected for life by a group of major superiors representing the different world-wide areas of mission in the Society. They in their turn had been named in office for life by the Superior General and were guided in the choice of her successor in a note, opened only after her death, which named the person she chose to be her 'Vicar General' and to hold her place during the interim period before the choice of the next General was made. In almost every case the Vicar General was herself chosen as General. In a very filial and conservative organization, this was a way by which change and movement were kept to the minimum, and the downward chain of command of a near absolute authority came from a considerable height. The Benedictines had only themselves as community to blame for their 'Christ figure'. The common of the faithful in the Roman Catholic Church and in congregations such as the Society of the Sacred Heart received their Christ-figures with great trust in the institution. As far as the Society of the Sacred Heart was concerned, the trust was justified and government was wise. But a situation of monolithic over-stability was the result.

Within each local community of the Society of the Sacred Heart the hierarchical concept was reinforced by reading every month in the refectory the 'Letter on Obedience' written by St Ignatius of Loyola in 1553. This tough recall to the Jesuits of Portugal reiterates absolute obedience to the Superior in 'that in which he is superior'. Even though the letter makes the obedience an obedience to Christ in a manner we could not blindly accept today, the phrase is important. Under the pyramidic pattern of the past there were certain things which a Superior could not command, above all under

the rare and solemn formula of 'Holy Obedience': that which
was contrary to the conscience of the subject, for example, and
that which was an act of heroism. This 'Letter on Obedience'
describes blind obedience: '. . . as, when the Catholic faith
proposes anything you instantly apply the whole force and
determination of your mind to believe it, so whatever the
Superior tells you, you should set about doing with that sort
of blind impulse which shows a will desirous to obey.' Various
desert father illustrations of this point were then given in one
of which a disciple being 'bid by his superior to catch a
lioness, caught one and brought her to him'. Someone once
pointed out that the right moral ending to that example
should have been that the lioness, so captured and brought,
proceeded to eat the Superior who had no right to command
such an act.

It is obvious how this thinking could be misinterpreted.
But it is not, after all, an act of faith restricted to religious
life. It was a submission of judgement expected from the
faithful by the Church and the use by Ignatius Loyola of the
Ptolemaic concept of the movement of planets round the
central earth, as an image of this kind of obedience, is apt.
The Copernican revolution, over which Galileo was
condemned, took till the mid-1960s to reach a Church still
operating psychologically, and expecting its faithful to
operate, in a universe of concentric spheres.

Of course the living out of this was very different from the
theory. The Christian freedom of the individual, the intelligent virtue of Superiors and the happiness, the well-being
of communities often resulted in a creativity which sought
and found the will of God in great joy and peace. The sum
total of holiness is neither more nor less under the systems of
Ptolemy or Copernicus. But the question is, and this is
important in a Church looking nostalgically over its shoulder
towards the neat obediential patterns of the past, which way
is more truly Gospel? Did Jesus show us a life which made
such submission of judgement a thing to be commended, and
by calling Superiors to 'take the place of Christ' were we, in
fact, giving them a power over their brothers and sisters which
is unlike the authority exercised by Christ? Jesus, who spoke
as one having authority, and whose passion throughout his
life was to do the will of the Father, did not tell his followers
to water dry sticks or catch lionesses. He did accept Peter's

request to be told to walk on the water. Is it sometimes we ourselves who ask to be commanded because we want to be seen to do the impossible? The call of Vatican II was to look to the Gospel. The obedience of Jesus, the exercise of authority by Jesus and by the leaders of the early Church must be our model. With this in mind we chose as a congregation to express something of our way of obedience in these words:

> Contemplating Jesus, whose food was to do the Father's will, who became obedient unto death, we learn to obey as he did, to give our lives for others. We surrender to God in faith, so as to be united with Jesus and to continue his mission.
> ... The way of obedience is a way of discernment, linked immediately to our call to contemplation. Listening to the Spirit, we seek to have a contemplative outlook on all reality in order to discover the will of God and make it our own.[2]

For my generation there was need to rediscover this way of Gospel obedience. I was as much a believer in the blue-print of God's will as anyone and as ready to see that if I struggled to obey, no matter in how absurd a situation, my desire to do that will would in fact be the doing of it, and the responsibility for the absurdity, the superior's. I also felt that if the Church laid down rules, the obeying of them was worth all the unnecessary suffering that resulted. I could, for example, in theory at least, understand the dilemma of the Jehovah's Witness refusing to allow his dying daughter to have a blood transfusion. It was crazy but his faith was real. Many things asked by the Church were very nearly as crazy, but I chose to belong to that Church. If I saw that something was asked by my Church, or I believed that was asked by my Superior, it would have seemed to me part of my Abraham faith simply to 'obey'. Then either God would work a miracle, or if he did not, death or suffering were preferable to 'disobedience'. No one believes that it is objectively wrong to eat swine's flesh, but the refusal by Eleazar or the seven brothers of the Maccabees to do so, choosing death instead, was, on my terms, admirable – and still is, because of the primacy of conscience;

---

[2] Constitutions 1982. paras 48, 50.

but is my conscience rightly formed by blind obedience? If there is to be a movement towards a true obedience it must be through a search for the truth. This is more easily explored in the microcosmic Church of a religious community than in the vast organization of the institutional Church.

A Gospel rather than a military obedience demands discernment. In a religious congregation this implies the search for the will of God by the individual and the Superior, the readiness of both to change in the course of the search, and a preparedness on the part of the individual to see that in this instance, he or she may once again be asked to lay down life for the brethren. The context of obedience – the Church or the congregation – is wider than that of private life, and the vow commits us to responsibility within this wider context.

The theology of this is Gospel, but a Gospel opened to new insights. How did Jesus obey? Whom did he obey? How did he discern the situation so that events and people spoke to him of the Father? My understanding of the Gospel, and that of many of my contemporaries, had to change, to accept a Jesus who did not necessarily know but who sought to know. Time was needed to allow the teaching of Vatican II to catch up with our experience of life, and for me, part of this coincided with a period in which I was asked to exercise authority. I believe myself called to be Christ by baptism, and in this assumption of a particular responsibility I saw myself neither more nor less Christ than before, but as asked, for a time, to hold the tiller of a sailing ship whose course was dependent on the wind of the Spirit. It needed willingness, however, on the part of every other Christ on board, if its sails were to catch that wind.

I am glad to have had the experience of exercising authority during this time; it has made me see more clearly, if from a far distance, the problems of bishops, archbishops and even popes. It has confirmed me in the belief that the Spirit is not finally frustrated by the human mistakes of those who hold the tiller, but that a way of growing in obedience to the Father together requires a listening heart on the part of the final authority. My impatience has often blocked discernment, but when there has been a true search for the way ahead, the

experience of obedience is profound. Then individually and
as a body we can say, 'Let what you have said be done . . .'³
The most emotive of the vows today is poverty. It always
was. My wartime noviciate was materially very poor and very
hard, but somehow we were always talking about how much
too comfortable we were. The first year after I left the noviciate was spent at the newly founded school at Woldingham
during the cold winter of 1946–47. The war might be over
but everything was in short supply. We had moved into a
large country house not only damaged by its wartime occu-
pants, but which had to be so altered that even such walls as
happened to be standing needed to be knocked down. Heating
and hot water were rare luxuries, and whatever there was of
either had to be preserved for the children in the school.
Meanwhile my fellow rebel of noviciate days and I were
working hard and at the same time grumbling hard that we
were not really *poor*. I cannot, from my upholstered old age,
remember what we felt to be superfluous under those conditions, but our infuriating idealism must have discovered
something.

I had charge of a group of the smallest children, and used
to have to wait for my breakfast until they were up and ready
for theirs. I would then go down to the basement where, in
a makeshift community refectory, late breakfast would be
prepared. This was meagre, but a delicious steaming bowl of
coffee was the lode-star of those mornings, when we had
already been up praying and working for a considerable time.
Alas! the day came when a sister refectorian with napoleonic
organizational skill decided that it would save time to pour
out each bowl of coffee before the late breakfasters arrived.
Some, and I was among them, were later than others. So cold
and skinny coffee joined forces with cold and lumpish porridge
as the flying start to a long, long morning, and I groused my
way through a month of such breakfasts. One day in mid-
grouse, the word 'poverty' seemed to slip into my stream of
consciousness with a sort of quizzical question mark.

That moment of truth has been a useful measuring stick
for all my personal anxieties about poverty. Whatever we
have as nuns is too much if we are thinking about the poor,
and whatever we lack seems to be the cause of complaint
made inwardly in the past and vociferously in the present,

³ Luke 1:38

even as we impose our private idealism on others. And yet our instinct is right when it tells us that without a real poverty we cannot claim to be followers of the poor Christ. But I see now that those days of material hardship were perhaps a blind to our search. We felt that if we suffered deprivation at the level of what we needed we were a little bit poor. We were, but to be so could stop us looking more honestly at the kind of poverty we were called to live.

There must be two aspects of living out this vow. The deepest and most important is the dispossession of all things, the unselving which calls forth the 'I am naught, I have naught, I desire naught but One' of Walter Hilton's pilgrim on the way to Jerusalem. It is in the contemplation of the hollowed crucified figure who even in death and after death suffered being 'done unto' as the last blood of his body was poured out at the hand of another. We who have asked the Lord to be with us know that there comes a time when we have to be with him in the acceptance of being handed over, stripped, an object rather than a subject.

We know that our lives are very far from our declared desire to be truly poor in this way. So we need the second aspect, the physical gesture that tries to say in our manner of living what we have said publicly by our vow, and what we want to want in our hearts. In the former way of an enclosed and habited life the outward sign was both given and not given. We possessed nothing of our own. We lived very poorly, and no matter how vast the institution, or beautiful the setting, the place of the 'enclosure' spoke of poverty. Given that assurance we were able to be in close contact with those who were wealthy without the risk of ourselves adopting a standard of living that was unfitting for us. But we were also cut off from the possibility of choosing a way of greater sharing. It was all done for us. Certainly there were some amongst us who lived more austerely and many who lived their poverty with Franciscan freedom and joy, but we lacked the power to make and remake the act of trust of sharing all that we have with the community. And we were safely cut off not only from the standard of living of the wealthy but also from contact with those who could best teach us the way of poverty – the poor.

The clear symbols of habit and enclosure, which said we were cut off from the wealthy, were more ambiguous in the message they gave than we thought. An English religious of a congregation very like our own but without the restrictions of enclosure, told of her experience in one of our convents in a Latin-American country. A long-established community, living in great personal austerity, could not believe her when she spoke to them of a shanty-town on their doorstep. They could only say: 'You are mistaken, no one lives there. No one could live there.' In the way of life that is theirs today they are out there, sharing the life of those who were each in truth 'no one', and who lived where only 'no one' could live. This is surely the unambiguous outward sign of trying to live our vow of poverty in a world where its reality is brutal. We may not all be able to do so as physically and radically as some of our sisters do, but we cannot hold a crucifix in our hands without seeking the means by which the crucified of today will be able to touch our lives and change them.

What can I honestly say has been my experience of poverty, of genuinely being poor, during these long years of professing poverty? Have I in fact ever been poor? I find the answer to that quite simply: 'Of course, and increasingly, as I have come to accept myself as I am.'

Looking back at the physical hardship of the early days of my religious life is a salutary lesson in the good and the bad of avoidable physical poverty. It can lead either to complaint or complacence. In my late twenties, poverty meant that the religious were often badly housed, overworked, and underfed.

The 'good' in this 'poverty' was that schools were simple, that there was a warm relationship of shared life between the nuns and the children, and what was needed had to be worked for. The 'bad' was when this kind of poverty led to the discontented ruses of escape that belong to 'asylum' situations. It was an example of external poverty which was adopted or endured and labelled 'holy', because somehow deprivation was holier than possession. The resulting extreme tiredness, for those already carrying heavy burdens, was then canonized, so that to be anything other was to be ungenerous. This was a time when physical external poverty was present in my life, and my tendency to over-dramatize made it a matter for self-congratulation, hardly the end to which the vows were intended to lead the person vowed.

But at the same time, in the struggle to pray, to live and to work with others, a more real understanding of poverty began to grow. The stripping and darkness of prayer, the weariness in well-doing which was quite other than the physical exhaustion of doing too much, seem to me to have provided the better opening to that poverty which keeps the one who seeks God a beggar at his gates. For me that way has continued and deepened to include all the frustration of discovering my limitations, my neurotic fears, my moral cowardice, my clinging to whatever might cover my nakedness in mind and personality.

I have also known myself poor when I have been unable to do that which has been entrusted to me. I have known myself rich in my presumption that I shall get what I need, rich in my sense of proprietorship over ideas or plans or in my arrogant expectations of service.

Patience and poverty are closely linked; the 'suffering of divine things' is the way to acceptance of the Spirit as the one who moves and achieves in a manner contrary to all that I expect. I know, therefore, that I am more poor and a great deal more free when what I have carefully planned is taken out of my hands and thrown into a metaphorical wastepaper basket. Times of sickness are perhaps the nearest I have come to that 'solidarity with the poor' of current liberation theology, from which my life has so far been insulated. A hospital ward is a good place for discovering that poverty is not about lists of things that I should or should not have, but about sharing weakness and fear with others and about being powerless, handed over to be 'done unto'. But above all to be poor requires a conversion of heart so that in union with Christ my life may proclaim freedom from things, in a world in which all should be for all. The great hymn of Philippians expresses it best:

> His state was divine,
> yet he did not cling
> to his equality with God
> but emptied himself
> to assume the condition of a slave,
> and became as men are . . .
> he was humbler yet,
> even to accepting death,
> death on a cross.[4]

[4]   Philippians 2:6–8

This way of Christ can be experienced very painfully in a sense of empty uselessness and in a certain bereavement.

It is also experienced in the realistic acceptance of the human condition, for the hollow Crucified is also the Christ of *Godspell* who stretches out his arms and allows himself to be pinned against the wire-netting limitations of being human. This is perhaps where the religious who has taken the vow of poverty has something to share with the whole Church, the Ecclesia. An old lady of great courage once said to me that she wished to accept voluntarily that which other old people had forced upon them, loneliness and uselessness. Through the vow of poverty, we religious, at every age, should be saying by our lives that we accept voluntarily what others have forced upon them.

There is something else which is perhaps even more important. Poverty should free the child in us, and as with Francis of Assisi, allow us to celebrate life. It will free us from the harness of giving and doing and lead us into the way of being and sharing and receiving, because we are in the end not what we give but what we receive.

Because of the person I am, the vow of chastity has always been central for me. It is the vow I have never had to rethink, and it is the aspect of the vowed life that makes poverty and obedience integral to the gift of life. But response to the call to live in this way has often wavered, often been tangled in conflicting calls to love, and for long stretches at a time seemed a charade, the cover-up of an inability to love anyone. But in spite of all this I know that the 'Yes with all my heart', reaffirmed, makes the only sense I know.

When I was a novice I had a private joke with God, that should I ever be called upon to write an account of my following of Jesus, it would be published for the world under the title of *The Way of the Mongrel*. This was partly because the chair-backs against which we would rest our hands in our stable-loft chapel made only one prayer position possible – that of the dog with its nose on its paws. The position was a good one for the mystic state of total stupidity, with a rampant imagination doing the rounds of the dustbins. At least in the time of recall to his presence I was comforted to know that I was still there, rather than tearing about the countryside scuffling in the rabbit-holes of memory. We used to return to this joke, he and I, when the remembrance of a call to lay down my life seemed pretentious or even blasphemous. Obediently and foolishly I would then be able to say to him, in and through and with his 'hollowed' son, 'This is my body given', and at least want to mean it.

Books on religious life often describe the non-relational living-out of commitment in the orders and congregations of men and women religious, and for most, the references to the vow of chastity in rules and constitutions were brief. In our rule the not entirely helpful call to imitate the purity of angels, which was lifted wholesale from the rule of the Jesuits, had the addition 'even the purity of the heart of Jesus'. This certainly gave an insight into fullness of loving and fullness of humanity. Now, although good things have been said in our revised constitutions about the vow of chastity, nothing has altered my own understanding of it, and nothing could go further than this 'model' of Christ's heart. But the understanding of what it is to be truly human has deepened, and the lifting of taboos on all mention of sexuality allows for the explicit statement of what celibacy demands.

My own experience was always of warm and real friendships in religious life. My school days' sense that the nuns were women of wholeness as well as holiness was not disappointed in the reality of community. At one time I would have said that all women were meant to be mothers, and that nuns were not exempt from this. I had met nuns who were spinsters in the pejorative sense of the term, and married woman with children who were even more spinsterish. So it was not to the physical fact of childbearing that this dimension of wholeness belonged but to what I felt to be a woman's need to foster life. But a fellow religious disagreed with me and said that women were meant to be those who loved and were prepared to be loved, and that it was in this that fullness of humanity came. She was right, and it is both women and men of whom this is true. Wholeness will come only to those who love; and love, of course, is lived in relationship whatever the context of a chosen way of life.

In my theory that religious life for women is in a special way an image of the Church, the vows symbolize the changes in the Church's relationship within itself. The way of obedience has been seen in as different a perspective as the world before and after Copernicus. The vow of poverty is made real in its recognition of Christ poor, not as one who demands help, but as one who calls for justice from the heart of the dispossessed. But the way of chastity remains mystical, and needs the affirmation of loving to make it credible. It is a call to accept the power of human loving as the sign of a covenant that is bridal, and it belongs to both marriage and celibacy. In celibacy the need for true self-love and self-acceptance is sometimes forgotten, while in marriage it is supplied by the unconditional loving of the partners. For the celibate who has no right to expect such unconditional exclusive human love, there must be an experience of and an inner assent to the love that is God. The self-value that comes from this is the key to a way of integration without which there can be no holiness.

A few years ago I was in retreat and becoming more and more aware of the shadow-self I disliked, and always experienced as my spoilt-brat ego or my mongrel self of noviceship days. One night, praying in a small oratory I tried to meditate on the parable of the Good Samaritan. My director had suggested that I see Christ as the Samaritan and myself as the traveller beaten up and lying in the ditch. I was unable to pray or think. Face down on the floor I itched from top to toe, and then, remembering my noviciate, I found myself telling the Lord that if he were coming to rescue me, it would have to be to rescue the mongrel, and that oil and wine were inappropriate in such a case. Suddenly, across my flippancy the whole scene changed to the resurrection encounter at Tiberias and Jesus was saying, 'Do you love me?' 'Do you love me more than these . . .'[5] and I was aware of all my dispersed and ego-inflating loves. In confusion, happy that there was nothing hidden from his knowledge, I could only say wordlessly, that he knew it all. And then it seemed to me that I looked over my shoulder at the mongrel who was also the spoilt brat and asked, 'What about her?' The reply to Peter was the reply to me about myself: 'If it is my will that she remain until I come, what is that to you? Follow me.'

Through acceptance in love of the spoilt brat of whom we are ashamed, I see a way by which the vowed life could speak to the world of today. Accepted, the brat becomes the child, the prophet of the Most High. Within each of us poverty will free the child, chastity will love this child, and obedience will

[5] cf. John 21:15ff.

lead this child to walk in the Spirit, responsive to the will of the Father. The hollowed Crucified will become the one whom the Father has raised up to be Lord of the dance, Shepherd of being, and he calls us to be with him as liberators in this world of destructive sadness, because we have accepted his liberation of our own destructive selves. Let us then dance and mourn to the pipes he chooses to play and, having nothing, know that the world is ours; bound to him by our loving, let us know ourselves truly free.

In an earlier chapter I found myself saying 'poor old nuns'. Here I want to say, 'poor stuffy, organizational, bureaucratic Church, so ponderously concerned about your dignity and your masculine privileges. You make such a burden of celibacy, such a sin-tangle of obedience, and to whom do you really listen in your anxiety to over-protect us all? To the poor who have no voice, or to the powerful who tame you to be an extension of their paternalism? Know yourself whole, and know yourself Ecclesia, at once bride, and mother, and child, one with the Wisdom who plays in the dawn of creation and who loves to be with those who are open to her teaching. Let us, as women who are nuns, prophesy to you by lives which try to make legalism into relationship, and which try to live out, in the microcosm of community, a wholeness and a dependence on the Spirit which is your greatest gift to struggling, searching human kind.'

8. Heart on the Outside

If the poor, stuffy, bureaucratic Church which I seem to blame for so much is to become whole, then each one of us must recognize that we are 'church' and are a dwelling-place of God. The words of the liturgy of the Mass for the dedication of a church should not be seen specifically linked to the consecration of virgins: 'This is a place of awe; this is God's house, the gate of heaven' declares a potential breakthrough place of God that is offered by every human person. I could say every 'baptized' person but who knows who are the 'baptized'? The mystery of every knowing, loving, existing person is a call to 'put off our shoes'. At each encounter with another we are reminded that the place where God is worshipped is neither on any particular mountain, nor in the temple of Jerusalem, but in spirit and in truth, here in this special place of indwelling, now in this moment of eternity. To worship thus, to live an adoration of awareness, is a continual prayer, a way of union with God which must embrace not only the other but the whole of creation. So to live is to celebrate life, and Jesus, the first-born, shows how this is our offered heritage, the way to the fullness of a humanity we share with him. We are all, potentially, worshippers in spirit and in truth, for only the human person worships, and only the human person seeks truth, or asks what it is, or repudiates its possible discovery. This implies that self-reflective dimension we call 'spirit'. Our destiny in Christ is to be translucent to the fullness of self-reflective being, God, and so to be fully ourselves, fully human.

I have a recurring fantasy: I am in a stream and the water flows through me changing me, modifying me. It is what Augustine calls the *nunc fluens* of time, or that *chronos*, chronological time, in which we find ourselves. In the stream I am still, held in the *nunc stans* of the eternal now, which seems to be sunlight illuminating the water. Even if my perception of that sunlight is through the moving water, I know that I am bathed in it, alive in its life, dependent on it for my being, more rooted in it than a tree is rooted in the earth, and more upheld by it in the now than the upward-thrusting, outward-reaching branches of that tree. It is a fantasy born of the experience of the passage of John 17, 'Eternal life is this: to know you, the only true God, and Jesus Christ whom you have sent',[1] that has been the door to prayer for me over the years. By prayer I mean that knowledge which is more than knowing, the knowledge, presence of relationship, of undefined kinship, the *sapida scientia* of the gift of wisdom and of the uncreated first gift, the indwelling Spirit.

Why these introductory reflections? Because religious are those Christians whose task it is to hold themselves open to the tranquillity more active than activity itself, that is God. Yet it is not a task, but in the very nature of whatever may be a vocation to the religious life, to live out that 'recognition of the heart' which makes each one say, 'I can do no otherwise'. Unhappily, not only in the apostolic congregations, but also in the monastic orders, either the structures set up to safeguard the priority of this call, or asceticism, or penance, or activity for the common good can take over. Time and space alone are the proof of the value given to any relationship, and the religious, 'eschewing all other', have made their central relationship with God in the now of today. But nothing Christian can be for oneself alone and therefore our awareness that this now, in this encounter, is the now of eternity, the meeting place of God and creation, will be an awareness shared. It will be seen in our loving and our freedom, not by peculiarities of dress or rigid patterns of life. It should be as recognizable as the ease of affection between husband and wife in a marriage that is real; it should be sensed in our company, communicated, not talked about, but perceived as the place of home-coming that each is to the other.

The alternatives between monastic and apostolic ways of religious life, or different apostolic ministries, are not the heart of religious service to the world. Religious profession should declare a presence and a priority, a shared call as human persons to a dignity beyond imagining. Why then so many

[1]   John 17:3

different orders and congregations? The Russian Orthodox Church with its far clearer conviction of the value of contemplative life, simply has one religious life. Our multiplicity of kinds and differing dedications make no sense in the Eastern tradition. It is sometimes felt, understandably, that we Western religious try too hard to convince others that there is something unique in the charism of our founder or foundress. The protest can seem too vehement and I have heard it suggested that we are convincing ourselves, reassuring ourselves of our identity when we claim that the Church would be the poorer if the 'colour' of a particular congregation were lacking. If the gift to the Church is that of men and women who make living in the eternal now their business, regardless of what else they do, how does the particular slant of their vision affect their contemplative contribution to Christian life?

'Eternal life is this; to know you, the only true God, and Jesus Christ . . .'[2] The contemplative who finds a deepest self and knows that self to be beloved of God, reborn of water and Spirit, discovers an identity, is one with the Word and is called by a name 'known only to the one who receives it'.[3] If this is lived, an aspect of the risen Christ will be manifested because a conscious drawing to a particular facet of the incarnation is experienced – to its hiddenness, its childhood, its brokenness or to the relationship of Mary with her son. A founder or foundress may find that this personal attraction is shared by others, and so each becomes more truly 'Church' in being one of a group who are gathered together because of a shared insight that becomes their gift to the Church. This opens for their fellow Christians a way of contemplative knowledge of Jesus, a way of going to the Father through Jesus, that both canalizes and widens for others the perception in the Spirit of who is the Father and who is the Son.

Once again I can only look at this through my own experience in my own congregation, but I do so, convinced that each group of contemplatives, whether they be monastic or apostolic, are called to be truly Church, truly Ecclesia, in a way that enriches the whole body. The multiplicity of dedications is therefore good. Just because the fundamental oneness

---

2 John 17:3.
3 Revelations 2:17.

of religious life is contemplation, there is a profound value in sharing the fruits of that contemplation, showing the marvellous variety of ways in which the incarnation can be apprehended.

In writing of the Society of the Sacred Heart, I have so far looked at the institutional aspect; and whenever the question of spirituality has come up, the indwelling Trinity and the Eucharist, rather than what the average Roman Catholic envisages as the Sacred Heart, has been stressed. Statues of the Sacred Heart belong to the folk art of Catholicism, and they tend often to disgust rather than to inspire. To have 'devotion to the Sacred Heart' was often referred to in my youth, but gave me little inspiration. The statues seemed to me merely statues of Jesus with the heart superimposed in order to emphasize the fact that he is love incarnate.

But there was a moment before I made my final profession when I became aware that the explicit reference to the Heart of Jesus throughout the constitutions of the Society meant that I could not evade the challenge of a particular symbol which, at that period of my life, I happened to find distasteful. It was not good enough simply to protest that what it signified was the Person of Jesus, or the Love of God made man. The symbol said something more or it was not a valid symbol, and if this were so, what did my consecration in a congregation for which the name Sacred Heart meant everything, mean to me? I realized that I had to read the image of the stylized heart as though it were a cryptogram, and discover in it what it added, for example, to a representation of the soldier's lance, piercing the side of the crucified Jesus and pointing to the moment of birth of the new covenant.

In order to explore the symbol I took as unattractive a pious picture of an early 'Sacred Heart' as I could find. For those who have never been exposed to this kind of representation, some sort of description is necessary. Based on the private revelations made to a seventeenth century nun of the Visitation order, St Margaret Mary Alacoque, the symbol of the Heart of Jesus became popular as a reminder that the incarnation was about love and salvation, not about retribution and the punishment of sinful humanity. In the form that I had chosen, it was depicted as a stylized physical organ, with a stab wound in its side, surrounded by a crown of thorns, and fire, and surmounted by a cross. It was the symbol that had spoken to the hearts of post-Reformation Catholic Europe grown cold and frightened by Jansenism which was the Catholic equivalent to Puritanism and whose self-scrutiny sowed the seeds of distrust in God, of fear and of self-condemnation among bewildered believers torn apart by wars of religion and by the scandal of a first century of divided Christendom.

The symbol of the heart, of course, went much farther back into the mysticism of Christianity than the seventeenth century. It recalls the beloved disciple leaning on the breast of Jesus at the Last Supper, the piercing of the heart on the cross and the appearance to doubting Thomas. It is present in the experience of mystics down the ages – Augustine, Bernard, Gertrude, Julian of Norwich often speak in terms of 'heart to heart' encounter with Jesus. In the eighteenth- and nineteenth-century Church the devotion, which spread with extraordinary rapidity, tended to focus on the suffering Jesus. St Madeleine Sophie, following the earlier seventeenth-century school of devotion, strongly emphasized the loving Jesus, the beloved Son. The primitive text of the constitutions and the 1982 version are a constant recall to this inner attitude which must be the focussing point of the Society, 'the glory of the Sacred Heart'. So love, glory, death, resurrection and a call to reparation, supported by a long history of mysticism, were somewhere in my mind as I held the particular image in my hand and asked myself what it had to say to me.

The result has been one of continuing revelation. The crude primitive devotional image became in a strange way a window in the wall of time, a meeting place of the *nunc fluens* and the *nunc stans*. Its very organic crudity said that the incarnation was real. Jesus was man. The heartbeat of the unborn child was his, and when his heart stopped beating he died. It was a symbol and a reality that signified the whole of his humanity, the whole span of his historical life, death and resurrection, his ever-living intercession for us, and his continued incarnational presence in the Eucharist. It was shorthand for what loving was. The surrounding thorns were more than just a reminder of a detail of the passion: they spoke of the mockery by men, the blindness that not only failed to recognize the King, firstborn of creation, but crowned him in this way. As I looked, those thorns brought to my mind the myth of Eden turned into a wilderness by sin. I found myself aware of my own power of mockery, and prayed, 'This is what we do to your gifts, to your beauty, to your person, whose greatest gift, after the power to love, is perhaps the gift of laughter.' Those thorns, apparently superimposed on the symbol, held me in a way that was totally unexpected. The cross that surmounted the heart is the Christian symbol above all others, the sign of victory and redemption, and the flames, the fire of Pentecost. Surrounding the whole were rays of light, a 'glory' which symbolized the mysterious fact of resurrection for us all. The heart of the risen Christ promises our own continued humanity, and opens the way to 'giving glory' by being alive ourselves in the one man who was fully alive. Alive, but killed by men, and I saw in that heart how he continues to the end of time to be killed and mocked in us and by us.

I found myself drawn into an awareness of the mystery of the person of Jesus. A response given to the 'Who do you say that I am?' could be 'Who do you, Jesus, say that you are?' and his answer be the symbol of his heart. This symbol-answer would be understood not only by 'penetrating the wounds of the suffering and dying humanity in order to learn the secrets of the divinity'[4] but by penetrating the wounds of all humanity, acknowledging myself to be one with the wounded as well as one with those who wound. The symbol seemed to be an invitation to discover a way of transforming compassion, a way of putting on the Lord Jesus Christ[5] by putting on the other, whoever that other might be.

In those days the idea of reparation was closely linked with that of devotion to the Sacred Heart and in confronting the image I would have accepted the idea in the literal sense of trying to 'make up' by love and fidelity for the blasphemy and infidelity of 'the world'. The importance given to the idea of reparation was shown by the consecration of the world to the Sacred Heart, and by the popular devotions that flourished everywhere. From it grew the desire to love more, to do more. Hearts were touched by the symbol of a reality, and the symbol became part of a folk religion, cheerfully freed from the constraints of good taste and from a Puritanism that looked fearfully at self instead of confidently at Christ.

As time went on the symbol itself became catalytic in my

4   Albert the Great.
5   cf. Romans 13:14.

understanding of the incarnation, and my acceptance of the idea of reparation was shaken out of its assumption that we, the virtuous, made reparation for sins committed out there in the blind wicked world. It was catalytic to my understanding of justice as I came to question the shock at an act of desecration of the blessed Sacrament, compared with mild expressions of regret in the face of human oppression. It was catalytic in my vision of the created universe – those thorns again became significant as the thought of our destruction of nature, our exploitation of nature, became part of the vision of the world we crucify.

At a time in the early 1960s when the unquestionable began to be questioned, I continued to hold that heart, in a very simplified image, as a mandala in my prayer, and its significance as a cryptogram of the shifting perspectives of incarnational theology grew stronger. Like the Greeks who approached Philip,[6] we religious of the Sacred Heart sought to see Jesus anew. We realized that we must go on discovering him, seeing him with the eyes of today, and knowing that our contemplation of his pierced heart would show us the Father and the world he loved so much. This was expressed in 1970 at the end of a General Chapter:

> To contemplate his heart we have no need to turn away from this earth, the home of God made man. Christ is present hidden in the heart of the world. Earth could not hold him in death; he lives and the whole world of time and space is transfigured through his risen life. He is present in the unconscious waiting of creation in travail; he is at work in the efforts of man to build a world of justice and brotherly love. It is in this very humanity whose fear and loneliness and love he shared that his GLORY must shine forth.[7]

Glory and adoration are two important words in the spirituality of the Society. They are therefore important to the particular understanding of the incarnation which is our gift to the Church as a congregation.

One definition of glory is 'full knowledge joined with praise'. Only the Father, therefore, can glorify the Son, and the Son the Father, because each is fully known only to the

---

6   cf. John 12:20ff.
7   Chapter Documents 1970.

other. The Trinitarian life is the relationship of self-giving and receiving, in a knowing that is Person and through a loving that is Person. The heart of the Man who is that knowledge, that self-awarenness of God made flesh, gives hope to the ache of human loving. As we look at it we can say that this is how human loving longs to be, to give all that it is, not only in death, but beyond death. We cannot have perfect knowledge even of each other, let alone of God, but we can praise, adore, and allow ourselves to be transformed 'from glory to glory as by the spirit of the Lord'[8] as we look on him whom we have pierced.[9] In the reality of life today our gift to the Church as a congregation must be to open ourselves to this transfiguration, to this 'knowing' that is of the heart, to this wound of knowledge that is a way of transforming love. This will be to live the glory of his heart and respond to his prayer 'that the love with which you loved me may be in them, and so that I may be in them'.[10]

In the first chapter I referred to E. I. Watkin's *Catholic Art and Culture* as a book which influenced me, and continued to influence me because of the hope it gave of a future age in which all Christians would discover their baptismal call to be contemplatives. In his concluding chapter Mr Watkin quotes from *The Spiritual Journal of Lucie Christine*, a mystic who lived at the turn of the century. She sees a new age of the Spirit, heralded and prepared for by an understanding of the Sacred Heart as a cult. Mr Watkin describes it as 'an age of adoring love, an age of interior prayer', when 'the spirit . . . will make known his presence and operation in Christ's members by the contemplative adoration he will inspire'.[11]

I have used the word 'mandala' in speaking of the symbol of the heart, and of the need for openness in the West to Eastern mysticism. The insights of Zen have been important in the search for a contemplative life, and the personal integration found through Indian spirituality has had a profound influence on prayer. As a Society we owe much to our Indian province in their exploration of Hindu spirituality and to the way in which they have shared this with us. Prayer groups and meditation centres are being established everywhere and

---

8   2 Corinthians 3:18 (Douai version).
9   cf. John 19:37.
10 John 17:26.
11 E. I. Watkin, *Catholic Art and Culture* (Burns and Oates 1942), p.160.

point to a hunger for the absolute, the *nunc stans*, the *kairos* which is strong at a time when all material things may be swept away and the *nunc fluens* is felt as a destructive flood. The world that is hungry for faith must be shown that the Christian Church is as rooted in mysticism as the East, and that it is at the still point of the experience of God that the Christian, the Sufi, the Zen master, the Guru and the various Rabbinic schools of mysticism meet. Here words cease and God is known to be unknowable. But for the Christian the good news is that 'we have seen with our eyes and touched with our hands the Word who is life'.[12] The fourteenth-century mystic Julian of Norwich tells of her shewing:

> Then with a glad cheer our Lord looked unto his side and beheld, rejoicing . . . And with sweet beholding he shewed his blessed heart even cloven in two . . . And with this our good Lord said full blissfully: Lo, how that I loved thee, as if he had said: My darling, behold and see thy Lord, thy God that is thy maker and thine endless joy, see what satisfying and bliss I have in thy salvation; and for my love rejoice [thou] with me.[13]

This 'beholding' is lived in the Spirit (whose presence is discerned in its effects, just as the wind is seen in the leaves that move) and is met in what the Hindu scriptures call 'the cave of the heart'.

The effect of the charismatic movement in its various forms all over the world is a further sign that the cry of Moses, 'Would that all the people were prophets', could be fulfilled in our time. Where men and women join together in fellowship, praising in tongues, praying for the outpouring of the Spirit for each other and sharing their faith, much as the early Christian community must have done, the formal respectability of Christianity is confounded. I have been humbled and helped by charismatic renewal at the point where being a religious of the Sacred Heart has tended to inhibit the expression of Christian experience by inbuilt decorum. Through it I have been upheld in my faith by others and learnt the freedom of shared praise. To be open to renewal requires being prepared to be foolish and to let God be God,

[12] cf. 1 John 1:1.
[13] Julian of Norwich, *Revelations of Divine Love*, 10th Revelation, Ch. 24 (ed. Grace Warrack). Methuen 1901.

and the result is what Christianity is about, and what religious life should be about – joy in a community where each bears the others' burdens and heals the others' pain.

The barrage of defence put up by the wise and prudent against charismatic renewal recalls a commentary on the Office of the Sacred Heart published in the 1930s by the Benedictines of Montmartre. In it the words of Psalm 116, 'I will take the chalice of salvation and call upon the name of the Lord', are interpreted as a call to take Christ's pierced heart, the living chalice which we may offer in our praise to the Father. The commentator remarks that some may resist anything so fanciful, but addressing the resistant he says: 'Stop talking. Do it. Then in great peace, simplicity and love, see what the Spirit will show.'

There are two further readings of the cryptogram or mandala of the heart which are relevant here: one is old and the other new. The new is linked once again with the idea of reparation and was shown to me by a sister who had entered in late middle age. The changes in our way of life in the late 1960s and 1970s when she was already elderly, seemed to invalidate much that she had struggled to accept as a novice. During a retreat she begged God for light on where the Society of the Sacred Heart was going in its sudden evolution. She asked to be shown what had become of the call to reparation, an important aspect of her vocation to give up her independence when she entered. She told me that one word came to her in her prayer: Awareness.

The day she shared that insight was a day of the Lord for me. It is a further dimension of the equation of reparation with the work of justice, of which I have already written, because it allows each one of us to recreate the universe. In the old dichotomy of natural and supernatural, I would have wanted to speak of the contemplative vision seeing through the created to the reality of the uncreated. Now I want to walk in Eden, and by seeing things in their own reality, call them by name. By so naming and valuing them, by my awareness of them, I shall foster the fullness for which they were destined, so that Christ may be all in all. I am reminded of lines from G. K. Chesterton's 'Ballad of the White Horse' which describe Alfred facing the destruction of his world by the undefeated Danes. He is 'broken to his knee' and is praying on the river Island of Athelney when –

> All things sprang at him
> Grass and reed,
> and the grass grew to be grass indeed,
> And the tree was a tree at last.

As I grow in an awareness of all that is, I must hold it in my heart and be a bridge of recognition which restores it to its wholeness. To change the metaphor, this is one way to repair the broken wall of creation, the result of the destructiveness of the sin which is mine, and ours, as members of the human family. I write here of creation as though I mean the world of things: of plants and trees and animals and seas and fossils and machines and architecture and music and learning. It is all these and much more, but the personal, the relational considered in the chapters on community and education, belong to this way of awareness at an even more profoundly creative and reparative level. My prayer, as I think of this call to reparation, is that of Ezekiel, that my heart of stone be exchanged for a heart of flesh.[14] That prayer is already answered because the 'love of God has been poured into our hearts by the Holy Spirit which has been given to us',[15] and our hearts are therefore one with the heart of the Son, the firstborn of creation.

The second way is old and very simple. The symbol of the pierced heart of Jesus speaks of the reality not only of self-transcendence but also of the call to believe in and be reconciled with my wounded and human self. I need to love, be loved, and love myself. I need to forgive, accept forgiveness and forgive myself. If I am to be that centre of awareness through which the Love that is God may be experienced, then I must have faith in the Son of God who loved me and delivered himself for me, and will use me, paradoxically, to extend his limitless loving. When we meet one who has such faith, and who lives it, we know that we must put off our shoes as we are in the presence of a real person, one who has become the place of *kairos*, of communion and communication.

One such was Sister Marie Scoazec, an old Breton co-adjutrix sister who was famous in the community at Oxford. As I write this and think of the mandala, symbol, cryptogram and human reality of the Sacred Heart, and what ought to

14 cf. Ezekiel 36:26.
15 Romans 5:5.

be the gift to the Church of each of us religious of the Sacred
Heart, I find myself thinking of her and I am back in 1948.
I am a nun student, and duty-washer-up in the scullery, and
therefore I cannot see who it is that Sister Marie has just let
in at the front door. I suspect it to be the newest hostel-
dweller's newest boy friend. Sister Marie will have gone to
answer the door bell with her knitting needles pushed up the
front of her bonnet and sticking out over her old Breton blue
eyes like the antennae of a friendly Martian. The stranger
will have been let into the hall to be confronted by a large
and somewhat gaudily painted statue of the Sacred Heart. I
can hear Sister Marie launching into an exposition of its
significance – St Patrick's shamrock, the Blessed Trinity, a
pope or two and St Margaret Mary ricochet off him as he
makes for the stairs. Then I hear her throw-away curtain
line, no doubt aimed at his ascending legs: 'You see zat zee
'eart eet is on ze OUTside and zat is what I am for 'im. Zee
'eart on zee outside so everyone know zat 'e love zem'. She
was just that.

And we must be just that. In the light of the particular
consecration of our orders or congregations, we must live the
good news of the Gospel so that others will experience being
loved and called to love. If we are free with the freedom
wherewith Christ has freed us,[16] we must be prepared to give
our lives to free others, to live fully alive and fully aware of
what is the heritage of us all. We must be ready to question
and be questioned by the world and by each other in the
light of the Gospel's urgency. We must be ready to hear,
assent to, and spell out in our lives, whatever answers are
given to our hearts through the heart of the Word made flesh
who dwells among us in the now, where time and eternity
meet. We, not I, and not you. To be Gospel we need each
other, we need community.

[16] cf. Galatians 5:1.

9. I Need You

At the end of the last chapter I said that in order to be Gospel we need each other, we need community. There are many ways of becoming holy, but, in all of them, as Christians we are called to be members of one another. The old way of religious life gave us clear structures by which we should seek to live this, and it was a way of life in its pattern prophetic to its time. We know that a new prophetic way must grow out of renewed understanding of community where religious life for women always mirrored the Church. The past tense is now used deliberately. Part of the fear of the bureaucracies of the institutional Church, over developments in religious congregations of women, is because of the new forms that are being sought in community life. As a result of this, many congregations of women today reflect the ecclesial theology of Vatican II more nearly than is possible for the wider community of the faithful. This is inevitable. The institution of the whole Church can receive documents with joy, explore their implications in relation to real life, as was done in Latin-America at Medellin and Puebla, and still, even in the light of the insights received, be frustrated by the slowness of adaptation in so vast a body. The religious community, small, flexible, with nothing to lose except conservative respectability, should take risks, make mistakes and explore new perceptions of obedience to the Spirit, of sharing faith, and ways of supporting one another in an attempt to live conversion.

In the past the mirror image offered by religious life was clear but somewhat distorted, because the Church had allowed the concept of a people of God, a pilgrim people, to become a monolithic institution strongly resembling the Roman Empire. The present mirror image is the reflection of present uncertainty. It is a moment of choice. Our community life as religious could allow itself to be tidied up, and show a cosmetic change, which would be flattering to the bureaucratic Church, or it could, and should, go forward to present the Church with a prophetic model of Ecclesia. It is in community that religious women should have the confidence to show what the charismatic Church will be, rather than simply continue to reflect, with slight democratization, what she was as institution. This means that we accept the responsibility of searching for a way of life 'wholly contemplative and wholly apostolic', to borrow a phrase coined by a contemporary canonist.[1] It means that we try to live open to the Spirit in communion with each other. If we do, our life in community will be a sign of hope to the people of God and instead of unconsciously continuing to reflect an over-centralized Church, it will be prophetic of the new ways by which she may be present through God's people.

The Church is about salvation, wholeness and holiness. So is religious community. The orderliness, security and uniformity of religious communities of the still recent past supported the conviction that as a way of life, the religious one was not merely good, but the best way of responding to the Gospel, of being whole and holy. Why? The Gospel says that where two or three are gathered in his name, Christ is present; in the religious community there were considerably more than two or three who had come together. All were gathered, in deliberate, conscious choice, in Christ's name, and therefore whatever the institution, order or congregation, the kingdom was present, because all who accepted its discipline did so with a common vision of life concentrated on and consecrated to Christ's service. Join up, and holiness was to be yours, because though the manner of service and the colour of the commitment might vary, the gift of self by the individual lived out in prayer and expressed by the three vows, made each institution a place of convergent search for the perfect following of Christ. The search seemed to need to go no farther than the perfect keeping of a rule approved by the Church. 'Keep the Rule and the Rule will keep you,' was the axiom. As the rule tried to put into words the charismatic experience of the founder or foundress, and to enshrine and

---

[1] Jeanne de Charry, *History of the Constitutions of the Society of the Sacred Heart.* Rome 1975.

safeguard ways by which charity, the only truly more perfect way, could be striven for, that axiom had a certain truth. In the institutions there were always holy men and women, but their fidelity and holiness resulted from an encounter with God in Jesus, a self-discovery which led to continued conversion, not simply from keeping the rule. They were, because they had come to know themselves and to know God, free to follow not only the rule but the community prescriptions in the minutest detail, and did so for love. They also had the inner wisdom to know when it was appropriate not to do so. They were, and are now, the Easter people, the real Christians who make Christianity credible because they show it can be lived no matter what the external situation may be.

I shall never be able to repay my own personal debt of gratitude to the many of their company who have time and again set me free because they have been dismissive of my cluttered, dualistic, rule-of-thumb world of the sacred. Where there is a way of serving God by the book, the faint-hearted will always find reassurance in doing so to the point of enslavement. For this reason the Church and its mirror reflection, the religious institution as well as the whole and the holy, encouraged and fostered card-bearing members of the Pharisee party, as in fact do all groups with the opportunity of measuring the performance of others in rule-keeping games. As a paid-up party member I should know. I also know that we shall always be present in some disguise no matter what the structure of life. But every attempt to find a way of coming together that helps us seek the will of the Father as Jesus did, checks our proliferation as a breed, and this is what community life should offer us. If it does, and if within it I am freed to face myself and my phariseeism as I look to that Christ who broke himself to be our shared bread, I shall grow like him. I shall join the blessed company of those who over the years freed me and have been the 'heart on the outside' for me and for others. This is what religious life is about, as it is what the Church is about.

One area which has been stressed in other chapters but needs to be spoken of again is that of authority. The authority that held the whole together structurally and psychologically, in the religious community, was a form of enlightened despotism which exercised considerable power maternalistically or paternalistically, and this exercise was resented.

Christian authority had allowed itself to become confused with power, and therefore the crisis over authority in the Church and in religious life was a rebellion against the use of power in the name of the Gospel. Jesus spoke as one having authority and he exercised power over the diabolic, but he never used power to coerce, manipulate, or protect, let alone over-protect. The worst effect of power, even in its most enlightened use, is that it generates fear, and fear is the 'diabolic', in the sense of 'disruptive', that undermines Christian community, and blocks growth into wholeness and holiness. Community is created by the struggle of sinful, forgiven and forgiving Christians, to make the kingdom present in the muddle of today. It is never furthered by the games that the exercise of power encourages, and which turn it into a truth-avoiding, other-avoiding juxtaposition of persons. These games will continue to undermine true community outside the institutions as they did within them, because domination by power can take many forms. The resultant presence of fear is cast out only by prayer and fasting, not simply by re-patterning our ways of living. Holiness is the result of an encounter with God, therefore of a recognition of the potentially diabolic in myself, and a life of continuous acceptance of his promised salvation. Community in the past and in the present is the result of relationships that cast out fear because they are striving to live Christ's way of loving. This costs us 'not less than everything' as we face the temptation to dominate and to possess.

Salvation, wholeness, holiness and community could be lived in the pyramidic structure with an ordered freedom that at its best was as joyful as a dance, and I can remember many experiences of how good it could be. One such was during my undergraduate years at Oxford. In many of the externals the north Oxford villa, which was our convent, reproduced an order of daily events that belonged to the larger institutions of the Society of the Sacred Heart of the time, and the rules of silence and enclosure, the strict division of the day into prayer and recreation were only slightly adapted to accommodate the student nun. The tiny basement refectory reproduced the quasi-monastic order of seating and serving, and was the place where, hot from a scramble to arrive in time for a meal, the nun undergraduate read to the rest and performed the 'penances' that belonged to this almost sacramental centre of community life. But apart from this general setting, our life was open to the adult non-religious relationships we needed. The house was small, the community was small, and even though the co-adjutrix sisters spent some of their time within their own 'community', presided over by the Superior's assistant, we were far more a single community than was possible in the bigger institutions. As a result we were obliged to learn how to understand each other, forgive and support each other and rely on our interdependence.

Above all, however, this was a community of prophetic experience because we had a young, intelligent and free Superior who exercised leadership rather than power. The doors of the convent were wide open to the world, and contact with tutors, other dons, fellow undergraduates, visitors who came for no special reason, or came and stayed during vacations, was informal. We met each other on common ground and, better still, sometimes met each other outside the convent setting. This offered the possibility of facing criticism, not just at the personal, but also at the institutional level, an experience denied us in our normal lives. Nowhere else in my pre-Vatican II experience of religious life could the atheist, the agnostic, the crypto-Catholic, the convinced Anglican or the practising Jew meet us as friends, not only individually but as a community. I look back to so many with particular gratitude. Dorothy Bednarowska, of St Anne's College, heads the long list because she has been a friend to men and women religious over the years and has a remarkable insight into religious life. She valued the real in our life when she met it and also saw through the bogus as others see through plate glass. She certainly made me question objectively and without sentimentality what we were about, and challenged my pretentiousness by her own Gospel way of life.

What that Oxford experience pointed to was a community group small enough for real exchange between ourselves, and open to the world in which it found itself. It had relevance of purpose without being tied to an institutional work, and a leadership that was enabling rather than initiating or imposing. There was time and there was space for prayer, and time and space to explore the things of God together, and to change and be changed by each other.

The first move in the direction of such a manner of living as this came with the long overdue fusion of the two categories of choir religious and co-adjutrix sisters in 1964. This decision, taken in response to the Vatican Council, coincided with the abrogation of enclosure, and was the first great shot across the bows of the Society of the Sacred Heart's unchanging course. Everyone from now on, it was decreed, was to be called 'mother' and the habit adopted for all was that of the choir religious. The immediate result of this for community was good in the fact that what had been an anachronistic injustice was now ended, but bad because in the subsequent confusion there was loss of identity and security, as each institutional community became unmanageably large.

Less than three years were allowed for this adjustment. Then habits were changed to the post-Vatican II uniform, and all 'mothers' were to be called 'sister'. In 1967 the Society sent its delegates to Rome to a special Chapter of Renewal required of all religious orders and congregations by the Church after the Vatican Council, and we lived through an earthquake experience which transformed the pattern of our lives. The aftermath of that Chapter, which was one of conflicting loyalties, meant for many an experience of death which was felt in direct proportion to their former unquestioning acceptance of the *status quo*. For others it was the grain of wheat which, if it died, promised a hundred-fold harvest of new life, and they returned with new vision. But the foundations were shaken, because the Church herself called us to mirror her own new self-understanding in the microcosm of community.

Where was I when all this was happening? I was becoming slowly aware, thanks to those who tried to educate me, that change had to be far more radical than I realized. It was only in the late 1960s that I read *Asylums* by Erving Goffman at the instigation of one of my community. The shock of recognition at the placing of religious communities among orphanages, prisons, lunatic asylums, barracks and concentration camps remains with me. It was salutary reading. What should be done about it? Expediency led us to try out various experiences in how we lived, and to venture out of the institutions. We found ourselves seduced by a form of democracy alien to everything that had preceded it, and disappointing to those who had hoped for something more charismatic in response to the call to renewal. From a situation where the members of the congregation had no participation in decision-making,

we moved into one in which there were unreal expectations
of total participation. This was to be by means of democratic
structures which multiplied committees and commissions,
and with them the numbers of those who failed to be elected to
such prestigious groups. In the name of community, increased
numbers of committed, saddened religious experienced alienation and deep rejection.

Meanwhile many left the congregation, some because the
situation was healthily catalytic; they should never have made
vows but might have continued in a diminished half-life if
the changes had not opened the door to legitimate escape.
Sadly, some left because they did not give themselves the
chance to explore the reality of their response to the new.
One or two were the victims of the time, used because of their
virtue as authority figures without the experience or stamina
to support what was demanded in situations of extreme
tension. Others found friendship and love outside community
in a way that had been denied them within it. Every departure
was a wound in the body at a time of great vulnerability, and
meant the loss of many whose vitality and vision would not
be replaced. But out of this woundedness an idea of
community began to take shape.

At this time I was sent to be Superior in an institution
where the large community had been divided into small
groups within the large main house. Another off-campus
group was included in my sphere of doubt-filled jurisdiction.
This community was one of the earliest experiments in independent non-institutional living; it had evolved from being a
mini-institution to having a life and shape of its own without
a Superior. This was, needless to say, looked on with disap-
proval by most of the inhabitants of the main house. So I
found myself surrounded by good will and fear, faith and
judgemental attitudes, tolerance and internal destructiveness,
in which everyone was suffering from an overdose of the word
'community'. This was used as a weapon against whoever
might hold contrary views about its correct interpretation. As
Superior, I made every mistake in the book. I superimposed
my own expectations of shared prayer and shared faith with
bland insensitivity, as I faced the culture shock of dwindling
from safe domination as headmistress to impotence in a position of so-called authority.

The sign value of nomenclature is always indicative. In the

society of the Sacred Heart we were each now, like everyone else, to be addressed as 'sister', and in fact we had begun to move into an era of Christian names all round. I found myself answering to 'Reverend Mother', 'Mother', 'Sister', 'Prue', from the various members of my community who thereby conveyed to me their expectations of my leadership. I did my best to be all things to all women and failed dismally, except for one brief moment when a much-loved old autocrat told someone that I was not a Superior but a friend.

This was the answer. If only we could have believed then and could believe today in our call to friendship. Paul calls it fellowship, but Jesus used the word 'friend', and it has always seemed to me the most important of all human relationships, implying shared vision and mutual trust between persons who stand equal with each other across the barriers of age or education. It is the underlying and lasting relationship in marriage, and without it members of a family will simply go their separate ways. One of the joys of growing up is to discover that parents are now friends as it is for parents to find friendship with their children. I love the Quakers' official name, 'Society of Friends', and I believe that my own Society of the Sacred Heart will have understood its call to community when it discovers the way in which it can live out the committed fidelity of friendship, first in the community of its members, and then with all those with whom it comes in contact. If we have chosen to seek holiness and wholeness together I need you, the other. I need to hear what you think and be prepared for your reply to influence me, to change me, as the waters of the *nunc fluens* in my fantasy dream are changing me. I need you to create me in the here and now of the imperfect, unsatisfactory present. The words of Isaiah, 'Your creator shall be your husband',[2] once came to me in reverse – 'Your husband shall be your creator', and for the relationship 'husband' every relationship seemed capable of substitution. My friend, my sister, my brother, my father, my mother, and my enemy are each in their way my creator, and I am theirs. I cannot have five minutes' conversation with another human person without being in some way changed; how much more therefore shall I be changed and recreated by those with whom I share my life! I am open to such change

2   Isaiah 54:5.

only if I am listening and receptive and therefore obedient to the Spirit whose life is ours, and who speaks to me not only through what you say to me, but through who you are.

But to be capable of creation by the other, to be able to listen and to hear, demands freedom from fear, as I suggested earlier. The undermining of friendship and community by fear is the diabolic which impedes the symbolic of the call to be of one mind and one heart with each other and with Christ, the call which makes community into Ecclesia. 'What do you ask of the Church of God?' is the question in the baptismal rite, and the answer, 'Faith', could be equally the answer to 'What do you ask of community and of friendship?' If power misused causes the diabolic presence of fear, then we must learn to use the power of Jesus in its exorcism, and the power of Jesus is released by our faith. It is also measured by our faith in each other. If you are to be my creator and I am to listen not only to what you say but to who you are, I am faced by the truth of my Christianity which demands living faith in you as a person.

In a congregation such as the Society of the Sacred Heart we are aware of three kinds of community: that of the whole international Society, that of the province which groups together communities of a particular country or combination of countries, and that of the local community. The way of wholeness and holiness offered by the congregation to its members, which I described in the last chapter as its charism, is the facet of the incarnation to which the contemplative intuition of its foundress was drawn. This is its gift to the Church, but it is not a blue-print, even if the founding vision is both inspirational for later generations and is echoed by the sense of recognition that each one experiences in her own vocation. The response to her vocation by every religious of the Sacred Heart, from the initial 'yes' to the day of her death, is the living charism, the renewed vision, continuing and enriching the international community, and, through that community, the Church and the world. It is awe-inspiring to realize that I belong to such a fellowship and that my personal 'yes', supported in love by that of the six thousand or so others who are flesh of my flesh, bone of my bone and heart of my heart, is making present the 'yes' that is Jesus in the now of today.

Once during a celebration of the Eucharist at a meeting of

all the provincial superiors of the Society, I knew for a moment what this meant. As we received the chalice at communion I realized that between us we carried in our hearts, knew by name and as persons in their own responsive right, every religious in the congregation. We, who gave the chalice of salvation to each other and received it from each other, represented the many others who lived this giving and receiving. In the joy and suffering lived out in every continent we were truly one heart and one mind, a community of faith. I found myself thinking at that communion of those who were dying, those who had run the race and completed the course, of the old and the sick who blessed us and prophesied to us, the contented as well as the disillusioned and cynical. I thought of the new-comers and of those who were feeling their way towards religious life and of those like myself, who plodded on in the fog. And I knew that all were part of me, and that I could never be for myself alone. Was this the communion of saints that Christianity offers? I think so. Because it was an experience of particular community of the presence of persons known to persons, it made physically actual in a special way the call to be open to the whole community of Christianity.

I have often read Ephesians 1, verses 3–15, rejoicing in the triumphant description of what it means to be called and chosen before the foundation of the world. I find it almost overwhelming to replace the 'we' by 'I' in this passage, and as I read it I beg for the faith to believe that what is said of the Ecclesia is true of me, of the spoilt-brat me. It requires a leap in the dark of faith to believe that. If I can make this leap in the dark, knowing myself to be who I am, I must be able to make the same act of faith in the name of each of my fellow-Christians. This is easy. It is even easy to do so, as I did at that moment of communion, thinking about those sisters of the Society of the Sacred Heart who were in my heart and in the hearts of the other assembled provincials. The real leap in the dark, the real act of faith is to read the passage in the name of each member of my immediate community, each one of those with whom I live and share my daily subterfuge and selfishness. If I can do this and acknowledge the truth of it in honesty, then the impact of the way in which this is addressed to the community at Ephesus as 'we' comes almost as a relief. I have seen myself and the sister with whom I live at close quarters in the light of our calling as individuals, and the immensity of what this means is almost unbearable. But the ecclesial, community dimension of the 'us' and 'we' with its assumption that what is wanting in me will be made good by you fills me with hope for who we are and what we are about.

While I was writing this I remembered being with one of the most loved members of my community when she was dying of cancer. It was some years before Vatican II and though community was the place of our life and commitment, we did not speak about it as we do today. Mary Weikersheim was an Austrian, one of the great givers of joy who was 'the heart on the outside' for me and for many others. She was weeping, and when I asked her why, she said, 'It's because I shall never see the community again. Of course they will come and visit me one by one, but I shall never be with them when we are all together.' At the time I was confused, thinking of the occasions when I had avoided those community recreations which happened to bore me, using the disguise of unselfishness by volunteering for some extra job in the school. But I also knew what she meant, and I meet it now in the 'us' of the letter to the Ephesians.

It is far more exacting to live the 'we' and the 'us' of that letter to the Ephesians in the apparently structureless pattern of today's community than it was in the past. We have got to shape our lives so that we allow the other to create us. We seek a way of living discernment, and if we take this seriously it is a structure that is far more exacting than any conformity or timetable of the past. We seek a way of helping each other to listen to the call of Christ as we share our perceptions of reality: in the events of the day, the Scriptures, the way in which we have met him in others. We confirm the faith each of the other in prayer, and we try to give each other the space and the solitude we need if we are to grow in Christ. We strive to build friendship and fellowship, and the Eucharist is the sign of the absolute of our union with each other. That is how we want it to be.

And is it? It is the ideal and the ideal is sometimes realized. One of my sisters with whom I discussed this chapter suggested that its title should be 'lead us into temptation' because community, if it is real, will be like the desert of long ago, the place where the demons that we meet as we seek wholeness and holiness are found within ourselves. Those who fled the city did not escape them. We did not escape them in the monastic structures of the past, and we are still called to face them and name them in ourselves. There is little in our life as religious today that can give us the satisfaction of having fulfilled the law in externals, and unless we are prepared to be pierced to the heart by the truth of who we are in relation to each other, we shall live lives of boring banality.

There was a line in the summary of the primitive text of the rules and constitutions of the Society of the Sacred Heart which said: 'Its (the Society's) fate is in their hands, it may perish through their fault . . .'. This seems to me to be the present situation for all of us religious. If we truly seek God we seek wholeness and holiness, and we will not only command the devils of fear to leave us, but we will face them and discover whence they come. Our healing is in our own hands and in our faith in our sisters, as we accept being known and loved for who we are.

The signs of the kingdom are reconciliation, pardon, liberation, healing and the celebration of life. Men and women have always longed for these things, and they are the promises of Christ to Christians, the kingdom made present in the ordinariness of today. The mission of community is to live them, and to recognize the 'now' and the 'not yet' that is the paradox of the Gospel. Community must be 'patient of divine things' as each one accepts the redemption that is already ours, and yet needs to be worked out step by step. The faith that is a true sign of the kingdom is lived alongside the experience of unfaith; reconciliation and pardon alongside the existential fact of anger and failure; liberation, over against the involuntary but real manipulation by each other; healing, knowing that we are wounded healers, still perhaps capable of using a knife to kill. It is only in acknowledging our 'tattered integrity'[3] that we find communion with each other and only through our failures and small deaths that we can claim the victory of resurrection and conquer our self-defensive, self-destructive fears.

These are fine words that butter no parsnips as we look at our reality, but monotony and ordinariness are the way we

---

[3] John V. Taylor. A talk given in 1978.

can choose to live as people who are poor, and no longer sacred or privileged. It is in the differing ages and backgrounds and interests, nationalities and races, of the unchosen companionship of our fellow religious, that we can choose to live our celibacy, forging a relationship with each one, so that we are in our own way a Society of Friends, not a group of isolated, virtuous individuals. Above all, it is through the mediation of others, through the listening that being together demands of us, that we safely search for the way of the Spirit, and live obedience. This is reality, and it can sometimes be heroism. Our continued effort to live it may be the most significant gesture we can make, in a world bitterly trapped in attitudes of enmity.

My attention was drawn by one of my sisters to the oneness of the call to community and the call to prayer. Both are a call to love. Yet when our prayer experience is an apparent blank, we expect to hold on in the darkness of faith, staying with the seeming waste of time. We are told that only by doing so can we grow in the love which is the true end of all prayer. This waste of time, this holding on in faith despite the emptiness and uselessness, is hard to recognize in the call to community, but if it is a faith-response in prayer, it is as much a faith-response in relationship, and, as in prayer, it is the only valid proof of a desire to love.

There are many more areas of exploration in this question of how we should live as the microcosm of the Ecclesia of the future. One which is of great importance is the way in which we, as women, support, and at the same time learn from, our married sisters who are living the essential Christian community of the family. We shall not prophesy to the Church until we have shown that we believe in the equal call to holiness in community of married and celibate chastity. Another area of importance to us as apostolic religious is the need for a physical displacement from where our communities have been institutionalized. If we are to live the conversion from one way of community life to another, we cannot modify; we have got in some way to uproot ourselves no matter how painful the uprooting may be.

The visible, all-embracing, isolated and admired city built on the hill has changed in the last twenty years, through a series of experimental patterns, to an unremarkable at-home-ness in the place where other people are. King Alfred translates Boethius' description of that for which things are made, and to which they are drawn, as their 'kindlig stede', the homing place of their nature. That seems a good description of religious community and of the Church as the gathering together of the people of God. It is not yet the full home-coming, but it is the caravan that promises arrival, discourages settlement, and is a homing place on the way for those prepared to live untamed by convention.

10.   That Christ Be Formed

One of my contemporaries tells a story, linked, as so many of mine have been, to the time when she was a nun undergraduate at Oxford. Next to our house at Norham Gardens was a nursery school attended by academic tots. One day when she was returning from her morning's lectures in full old-time habit and university gown, an exceptionally donnish three-year-old, about to be collected from school by her father, looked at her and asked, 'Daddy, what IS it?' The embarrassed father muttered something which did not divert either the enquiring mind or the penetrating stare. Question two followed: 'What does it DO?'

During the past few years there has been an over-used cliché which claims that 'being is more important than doing'. Obviously it is impossible to do anything without being something, so that, in that sense, being comes first; but for a human person it is impossible to *be* without *doing*. Scholasticism taught that no human action is morally indifferent, but for an action to be human it must have the element of choice, albeit in many cases, choice conditioned by habit. Therefore the doing juxtaposed to being in the cliché should be human action, and for the Christian, must express outwardly something of the inward commitment to Christ of the one who performs it. If a smile or an outstretched hand belies inner murderous feelings, the smiler is either a hypocrite, or a saint who transcends these feelings with forgiveness and love. 'Doing', when it is expressive of a person who accepts the baptismal call to transformation in Christ, is sacramental, and that sort of doing should be indivisible from that sort of being.

The pity is that, for many Christians, the greater part of their active lives is spent in a doing which seems unrelated to this continuously transforming Christ-life. The Christian,

obliged to face the drudgery of impersonal and unrewarding
work, or the humiliation of redundancy or unemployment,
may, by his or her attitude to the evil situation, express Christ
very powerfully, just as may the Christian suffering disease
or facing death express a being done unto, which is one
with Christ's passion. These evils, and they are evils, are not
destructive of an outward expression of inner truth as is, for
example, the becoming enmeshed in the world of big business
and power in which doing is essential and choices must be
made. Today's Christian may be asked not to offer incense
to the god-emperor or to face the lions, but to decide whether
what is at hand to be done is, or is not, capable of becoming
a sign of the kingdom, in a world where nothing is black
or white and where many greys may be rationalized into
acceptability. Even more challenging to the Christian in the
secular culture of today is the choice to act or not to act
in the corporate situation: to oppose the destruction and
degradation of others, to fight for human justice, to be
political, or to walk by on the other side, afraid of
involvement.

Religious have, until very recently, been spared much
heart-searching about whether what they did was or was not
consistent with their baptismal consecration. The nineteenth-
century Church tended to hold itself aloof from politics. The
practising Catholic hesitated to dirty his hands with the business of government, and in a world that separated sacred
from secular values, the activity of religious was identified
with the sacred. The Church was once again reflected by the
citadel of religious life, which, with great relief, left the world
outside the door and concerned itself with a doing that was
of the spirit or with such works as spoke unambiguously of
mercy. Or so it would seem. But the Gospel shows that no
work of mercy is unambiguous or a-political. If it had been,
Jesus would not have been done to death.

Jesus taught and healed and liberated and challenged the
assumptions of the establishment of his time, and those who
have followed him through the centuries have done the works
that he did. They are known as his disciples both by the sign
of loving and by the sacrament of doing which declares the
presence of the kingdom: the blind see, the lame walk, the
poor have the Gospel preached to them. The Church prays,

heals and teaches, as do those who have committed their lives wholly to its service and to a close following of its Lord.

As long as the work of teaching is concerned with minimal literacy it may be seen as a work of mercy, and though by no means necessarily a-political, is far more easily sacrilized than the further and higher levels of education in which religious are involved. When teaching moves outside the sphere of preaching and beyond the basic skills it obliges the teacher to enter the secular city. It is therefore the way into a world of the complex and the ambiguous, and the religious who undertakes it has not only to make choices, but to lead those who are being taught into a freedom, from within which choices can be made. In the citadel Church, and the citadel religious institution, the religious educator has to examine the inter-relationships of different disciplines, and value his or her expertise for its own sake, following its lead with integrity and with an open mind.

When I spoke in an earlier chapter of the sign-value of what the pre-Vatican-II Church described as the 'mixed life' for religious, I said that it gave a double message. I suggested that for us, as the Society of the Sacred Heart, this was because it was equated with the Church of privilege through the kind of work it did. This was the work not only of primary, but also secondary and tertiary education, and though much education is not, nowadays, the exclusive possession of a particular social class, whoever is so educated becomes one of the privileged. Whoever educates is therefore already privileged, and is also obliged to rethink the dualism which divides life into areas of sacred and secular.

The Society of the Sacred Heart was always described as an educational order. We, as Sacred Heart nuns, would have strongly denied that we were an 'order' and we would maintain that formal education was only one of the principal means by which we tried to give expression by doing, to the essential reasons of our being. This being is union with and conformity to the Heart of Jesus, a oneness with him by which our lives are lived for his glory. The ways, besides formal education, of expressing what we are by what we do, were presented to the members of the Society from its earliest beginnings as the work of retreats, and 'any other means' by which holiness could be sought, not for ourselves alone but for and with those whose lives touched ours in relationship.

All these means were educative, and the formal education in schools was seen as a way of leading children into an awareness of their Christian call. So perhaps a way of expressing this being and doing might be, that holiness was the end and relationship the means, with the symbol of the Heart showing the inseparability of the two for the human person whose fulfilment is in Christ. Somehow that was what we had both to live and to communicate, and from the beginning of the Society's history the most immediately recognizable way by which we did it was by running successful boarding schools for girls.

My own experience of meeting Christ, of learning to pray, and at the same time discovering that I was not the unteachable anti-intellectual that I had thought I was, is the experience of many for whom the Society of the Sacred Heart offered, through the boarding school, a place of real education. I am also grateful to have served in the world of the old-fashioned boarding school under the restrictions of the pre-Vatican-II way of life, and I am glad that it was from within it that I lived through the Vatican II revolution. The theory that I have proposed, that the convent mirrored the institutional Church with extraordinary accuracy, is completed by the presence, within its citadel, of a school. To our being, which reflected the bridal Church, was added the reflection, by our doing, of the teaching Church. Those who were at the receiving end of that teaching, not only lived the revolution with us, but forced us to recognize that it was not simply the Church imposing change, but that the world itself had changed and it was time we recognized the fact.

I have described something of the life of the boarding-school world in various other places in this book. The temptation is to indulge in a 'do you remember?' because the shared experiences of nuns and children are worth remembering. Ivan Illich used the word 'conviviality' in the context of education, and it is the best I can think of to describe the vitality and creativity, the friendship and interaction of ideas and ideals of the period leading up to the early 1960s when we all seemed to speak the same language and when we explored ideas from the same safe starting-point. It was above all, and this was its greatest strength, an experience of community, a wide community which was able to celebrate life. But we did not see that we reflected the pre-Vatican-II

Church all too well. We were still educating out of a presumption that the answer to human questions remained unchanged, and that though argument and exploration were good, somehow, somewhere, answers were safely stored up for opportune production. I have compared the Church's world vision with that of the Ptolemaic solar system. So was ours, psychologically, and so was the language we were using, while intellectually we were operating in a world that was post-Einstein. We could not know that the result of this was not so much a new dualism, but a sort of schizophrenia.

Liberation theology tells us that there are a whole series of revolutions of the spirit in which the Church had no part, but with which it must come to terms if it is to speak Christ to the world. All these revolutions further the cause of human liberation, but from the scientific revolution through the bourgeois, the socialist, the atomic and the cybernetic, the Church has been either unaware, unconcerned, or in direct opposition to the process of emancipation. Succeeding generations of religious educators taught the historical and sociological facts, at least of the first two revolutions, but taught them as though they were great rivers swirling round the rock of Peter, which affected people but did not touch the Church. This was an unconscious but revealing distinction.

Now in the early 1960s, not only was the Church caught up in the river of change, but shifted out to sea by it, and simultaneously it seemed that the safe world of the young whom we were trying to educate, was increasingly separated from ours. The Beatle era had begun, and so had the teenage and television cultures, CND marches, the pill, the vindication of *Lady Chatterley's Lover* and the need to go about looking as though soap had yet to be invented. Each of these implied new social values where, in my early forties, I already felt out of my depth. The generation gap had suddenly yawned, and I was stranded on the far side of a growing gulf.

Education is dependent on communication. It was at this time that I became aware that I was no longer transmitting correctly from my inbuilt radio. Among the many friends and parents younger than myself who tried to further my education at this time I owe a special debt of gratitude to Dom Sebastian Moore. His book *God is a New Language* made me realize that we needed to learn that new language of God. But I was a slow learner, and was miles removed from the real and necessary shift in the basis from which my thinking started.

In 1967 I was moved from the boarding-school at Tunbridge Wells where I had been Headmistress for a number of years, to be Headmistress of the school at Woldingham. This was the successor to the Roehampton convent described with bitterness in Antonia White's *Frost in May* and with love by Brigid Boland in her biography *At My Mother's Knee*. I went reluctantly, feeling that I was too old to bridge the generation gap of which I was now acutely aware. I found, however, during the short time of my headship, that the sociological background of the Woldingham school had slowed-down change. Most of its children were still brought up in nurseries whereas the Tunbridge Wells children at that date were not. I left Tunbridge Wells on the eve of the spill-over of drug addiction into the classroom, and found Woldingham still a few days removed from it. I left Tunbridge Wells aware that I was not transmitting accurately to a large variety of receiving stations in the school, where most of the older members were rebelling against their families, and found at Woldingham that, by and large, there was still only one receiving station, and that therefore communication was clearer and more immediate. The child of the nursery tended to be more anxious to conform to the values of slightly distanced parents than the hand-reared variety. Both schools stood for something in which I believed, and I loved both, but the first years at Woldingham fostered an illusion that the generation-gap was not as wide as I had thought. It was not long before I had to face the fact that I was still unable to speak the new language of God. I was very happy in the school and was accepted as a reasonably adequate Headmistress, but I knew that as far as communicating the Gospel was concerned, even in 1971, I was no longer being heard.

We are back to the question of being and doing, and the search to make doing consistent with what we are. 'For the sake of one child I would have founded the Society' is a quotation from St Madeleine Sophie which is known by everyone educated in a school of the Sacred Heart. We, and those whom we educated, presumed that the one child should be drawn into an institution, because that was the sphere in which we, as religious could operate. When this was no longer the fact, we as religious had to make choices: where was the one child best reached? Was the attempt to preserve the total environment of the boarding school educationally better served by a religious community, given the fact that such a community was on the fringe rather than at the centre of such a school, and that the institution was no longer a place experienced as withdrawal from the secular world?

Institutional education was a particularly appropriate ministry, and a particularly successful one, for religious of the Sacred Heart in the days when religious life was itself clearly institutional. It created a world-wide bond between those who had been at home in it, linked them to a purpose far wider than the actual institution, and through the dedication of the religious communicated a sense of the ultimate. But then something happened to the institution in society at large as well as in the Church and in religious life. That which had been accepted as good, at least educationally, was now equated with depersonalization.

The schools and colleges we ran were a thermometer showing us what was happening in the world outside religious life. Those least affected by social change were of course the primary schools, which continued to be the places of growth for children that they had been, because they were places where home was brought into a school which was minimally institutionalized. The secondary day schools were also free from the pressures of total institution. If they were happy, their influence was great; if they were unhappy, the child subjected to their pattern of education escaped back into the real world outside as soon as possible. The Teacher Training Colleges of the past evolved into independence from the total institution. In the 1960s the single-sex quasi-boarding school Colleges became degree-giving establishments. In the 1970s these newly named Colleges of Education became in their turn co-educational Colleges of Higher Education and offered a variety of degrees, catering for students who now were adults before the law. The citadel of the convent therefore was no longer a place of total environment in relation to the students and therefore no longer a place where doing communicated being. This was in a measure also true of the institution of the boarding school.

One of the most valuable statements that the educator can make to the adolescent is that adult life works and is happy. The Christian educator should also be able to say that men and women, celibate and married, can work together and speak the same Christian values. The religious educator should show that adult life which is celibate for the sake of the kingdom is a life of real relationship, that it expresses its primal relationship to God in prayer, and that it is a commitment to living in a way that says space for God and community are essential to it.

I realized as long ago as the Tunbridge Wells of the later 1960s and the Woldingham of the early 1970s that we were no longer expressing this in a way that could be either heard or clearly seen by those we educated, however much the relationship of individual to individual might be strong, affectionate and revealing of Christ. It was certainly not a way of life those we educated wanted to follow, or saw as relevant in terms of the Gospel for today.

If I were a sociologist capable of drawing meaningful diagrams, I should express the educational wholeness of the total institution of the past as three triangles which fitted neatly into each other – that of the Church, the community, and the school or college. All three would be in part superimposed on the world, a separate circle. The education offered by the Society of the Sacred Heart was remarkably fitting in the shape of the three-fold triangle. It was coherent in its philosophy, it saw the child or young adult as a person to be given every opportunity for full development and treated each as an individual.

In the far-off days when a plan of studies could be shared by Sacred Heart institutions all over the world, that plan was a masterpiece of educational wholeness. When it was updated in the early 1950s it continued to offer an inspiring ideal of education which opened windows for those of us doing our best to be educators and finding great comfort in a strong and successful tradition.

But my next diagram would be of the time of transition: the collegial Church would be a circle as nearly one with the world circle as possible, and the religious community, democratized and uncertain, represented by squares, cubes and hexagons. The educational establishments, increased in size, will have grown outside the community, shaping themselves to the world circle, and no longer shaped by the community.

My third would be of the future – the Church present to the

world through the Christian community, circles interlinking within the circle. The religious communities would be there, and I find a shape and a place for separate educational establishments where they are Christian communities in their own right, serving and served by other circles of community.

I experienced something of this as a short-lived college Principal in the mid-1970s and I am therefore convinced of its potential. The religious community was interlinked with the community circles of academic, administrative and domestic staff, and together provided a setting where the student could freely discover Christian community. It was a prophetic pattern, realized far more effectively by my successor who showed how a place of formal education can become a centre of creative enablement.

But I am sure, having lived through my own congregation's movement from the quasi-feudal into a period of democratization of life and work, and then on into a search for a new and more Gospel understanding of community, that the work, the service we undertake, must be educational. It must be both a communication of the transcendent and the response to real need. This sometimes seems to be more clearly indicated in a Third-World situation or from within a Latin-American basic community, or shanty-town, or U.S.A. inner city, than in the England of today. Here we have become used to earning good salaries from the State in return for running excellent and needed educational institutions, whether they be primary, secondary or tertiary. We claim rightly that to run them is a work of justice, and that to teach in a university or to run a good independent school is in no way an injustice. Wherever we educate we seek to free the individual so that Christ be formed, no matter to what milieu that individual belongs. But for some amongst us there is dissatisfaction, discomfort, in our declaration of this truth. In the wide areas of choice that are now open to us, we have got to face the dilemma of choosing between the good things we are able to do. We have the duty to examine what we are already doing, and though we may find it the best we can do, we may also find ourselves led to make some radical choices, easier for us than for those who have neither community nor congregation to support them. We, as religious of the Sacred Heart, must look for that educational doing which is truly a sign of the kingdom in the confused context of our own affluent society, a doing which is relational and contemplative and which is sought for in spirit and in truth, not forced upon us by current forms of guilt-complex.

Ronald Knox spoke in one of his sermons of a '4 a.m. feeling'. One of mine was a cold-dawn realization that if every believing Christian in Hitler's Germany had put on a yellow star, Hitler would have been powerless to carry out his extermination policy against the Jews. Then, feeling like Abraham arguing with God, I found myself moving from every Christian to every Catholic, to every religious or priest, to every woman religious . . . Even if every woman religious had done so, the Third Reich would have been sorely embarrassed. That particular 4 a.m. was some time in the 1960s and I had to ask myself then what equivalent situation should we at that time have been facing. I could look across the Atlantic and say that at least in the deep South each Christian, Catholic, religious, priest or nun should paint their faces black. Shortly after this a remarkable book was published, *Black like Me*, in which John Howard Griffin told of his experiences in the 'deep South' as a white man who made himself look like a Negro. I found myself not only deeply moved by reading it, but also busy congratulating myself on my dawn insight into the true Christian call of the time – for the U.S.A. of course. Then I realized that I was not only projecting myself backwards to Hitler's Germany, with the wisdom of hindsight, but also away from my own situation to a distanced U.S.A. What was it that England called us to do in the 1960s and calls us to do today? Perhaps our sisters, the women of Greenham Common, are showing something of what it could be. But why then am I sitting here at a typewriter?

Other congregations are searching, as we are, for answers that will only be found in the doing, not in the theorizing. Other congregations will have their own patrimony of what has been in their former pattern of apostolate to build upon, to grow from. We cannot all do everything, but we need no longer be afraid of making wrong choices, of making mistakes in our search. As the Society of the Sacred Heart, we tried in 1982 to express the call to respond to the needs of the present, rooted in the experience of the past by seeing that:

The Church needs us to communicate the love of the Heart of Jesus. In him all find their true growth as persons and the way towards reconciliation. This we believe; this we want to proclaim.

St Madeleine Sophie chose to express this conviction through the service of education. Faithful to her inspiration and open to new situations, we make her desire our own – that persons become aware of their own power of love and freedom, discover the meaning of life and share it with others, be valued so as to make their own unique contribution to the transformation of society, experience in themselves the love of Jesus . . . let an active love shape their lives.

The urgency of today's needs and the call of our local Churches impel us to respond creatively according to the diversity of our cultures.[1]

I find myself content that this expression holds us to our contemplative purpose, and grows out of it. For us, education is to see the other so potentially alive that he or she may become more and more truly the glory of God. The words 'reconciliation' and 'justice' are pointers to what we must live ourselves and try to bring to life wherever we are. We are free now to serve the Church in the reality of where people are, and we are glad that, because of the educational opportunities of the post-war world, there is now no longer, in England, a gulf between the Church of privilege and the Church of the people; but there is a world which the Church does not reach, and as educators we keep it in mind.

Within ourselves there is danger of a new sacrilization, and a new hierarchy of values that would contradict what we claim to be our perception of Church and incarnation. In the institutions we pursued an excellence that claimed the teaching of 'secular' subjects to be as much of the Gospel as the teaching of what was then called 'sacred doctrine'. With Aquinas we claimed that all truth was of the Holy Spirit. In the new dispensation we are tempted to put work in a parish, the teaching of catechetics, the direction of retreats, degrees in theology, the running of religious-studies departments, or work as hospital or university chaplains at the top of the value ladder. Those who give their lives to the challenge of students in a purely academic discipline can feel marginalized or less prophetically involved, and this is dangerous.

[1] Constitutions 1982 Para.10,11,12,13.

If we believe what we say we believe about the incarnation, it is as important to value the teaching of non-religious disciplines as it is necessary for us to go out to work for justice wherever people are. This is our place of 'reparation' which is one with our call to educate. St Madeleine Sophie saw that deformation of mind and judgement are a tragedy as great as starvation. Our challenge to the Gospel therefore may well come from the highly articulate student-world through an academic discipline which stands in its own right as essentially 'secular'. Our contemplative purpose of education is always to liberate, to enable the other to see and to be, to question, to seek, and to choose that for which he or she is made – truth.

I owe my introduction to the following poem to Dr Elizabeth Templeton of the Divinity Department at Edinburgh University. She described it, in an article published privately, as a prophylactic *envoi* to the young who must grow up in the shade of Church/school/State/culture orthodoxies, and I quote it in full. If I were to give an answer today to the small child's question, 'What does it DO?' about one of my fellow-religious of the Society, I should love to be able to reply, 'It tries to say, mean, live this:

Children follow the dwarfs, and the giants and the wolves
into the wood of Unknowing, into the leaves

where the terrible granny perches and sings to herself
past the tumultuous seasons high on her shelf.

Do not go with the Man with the Smiling Face
nor yet with the Lady with the Flowery Dress . . .

Avoid the Man with the Book, the Speech Machine
and the Rinsoed boy who is forever clean.

Keep clear of the Scholar, and the domestic Dog
and, rather than Sunny Smoothness, choose the Fog.

Follow your love, the butterfly, where it spins
over the wall, the hedge, the road, the fence,

and love the Disordered Man who sings like a river
whose form is Love, whose country is Forever.'[2]

[2]   Iain Crichton-Smith, *Bourgeois Land*. Gollancz 1969.

Elizabeth Templeton wrote of this poem that it is

> a text which fuses what I would like to do as a teacher and what I find central to my theological nervous system. I want to give people the room to explore as richly and freely as possible the strangeness of the world, and I suspect that a condition of that exploration is that one should be an outsider to whatever system of exploration is standard practice or current orthodoxy.

This is an important sign-post. I have suffered, and still suffer, from many self-blinding illusions, and one of them is that I have never been conventional. Now, as I look back at myself as an educator, I see that the conventional was present in all my attitudes. In the 1960s I should have listened with appreciation to the call to come out from behind the conservative barriers and speak the new language of God, and in the 1970s I should have applauded those who did. Now in the 1980s I believe myself at last beginning to be ready to discern the unorthodox choice.

Christianity is always being tamed to fit the acceptable social pattern, and the institutional Church has been mirrored by the institutional convent running the institutional school or college. This was always in danger of being the place of conservative conformity, especially when it belonged to the Church of privilege and was concerned mainly in educating the privileged. But today we may be trapped into new apostolic conformities turning away from the disciplines that are secular as though they were unfitting to our call, if we are motivated by guilt and not by love. For that reason I should want us as religious educators to help each other recognize, point out to others and

> . . . love the Disordered Man who sings like a river
> whose form is Love, whose country is Forever.

in whatever reality he may seem to hide himself.

Epilogue

In the early 1960s I first saw a film called *Parable*.[1] It was a twenty-minute mime and opened with shots of the wagons of a circus and fair on the move. There is a long train of these, brightly-painted, labelled according to different countries of the world, horse-drawn or elephant-drawn or llama-drawn, and they wind their way along a lakeside road, framed in the colours of a North American fall. The folk-art decoration of the waggons seems to use inset mirrors, the idea of reflection is caught up in these and in the polished harnesses, and in the lake itself. Behind the waggon train, taking the crown of the road in freedom, rides a white-clad clown on a white donkey.

The next series of shots is of a steep drop through trees to the lakeside. A man is lugging two full pails up the slope from the lake, with which to water the elephants. Clearly a 'hewer of wood and drawer of water', he struggles with them as far as he can, puts them down, and sits exhausted with his back to them. And the white clown is suddenly there behind him, a strange tall figure with a whitened face, looking down at him with an expression of utter compassion. The impact of the clown's appearance is at first almost one of fear. Certainly it brings a shocked question mark into the mind which, without being answered by recognition – oh, that is who he is meant to be – is replaced by a movement of the heart as the camera focuses on his face. Then there is quick action. The clown picks up the buckets and strides up the hill, the elephant-keeper jumps up, at first bewildered, then indignant,

[1] *Parable* (Rolf Forsberg). Film released and copyrighted in 1964 by the Protestant Council of the City of New York. Available in England from the Evangelical Film Fellowship, 67 Linnet Drive, Chelmsford, Essex CM2 8AE. Used with the permission of the Protestant Council of the City of New York.

then scrambling after him astonished and grateful. But the clown does not stop or explain. There is a brief shot of the tethered elephants as he leaves them their water, touches their trunks with love and walks swiftly on to the fair-ground. The next shots are of various acts of liberation. The first concerns the man at the entrance of the circus fair-ground. The impression given is of tickets being sold by a con-man to crowds pressing at the gate. And the clown is again suddenly there, listening, then ducking under the barrier, getting hold of ribbons of unsold tickets and throwing them away free to the people, and going on his way. The man at the gate becomes his first enemy.

We follow the clown to a side-show where a sad Negro, sitting on a ducking-stool, waits to be used as a human coconut-shy. Beneath the ducking-stool is a trough of water, surrounding it a wire cage to catch the wooden balls that are to be thrown at him. The object of the game is to hit the Negro so that the winning ball triggers off a mechanism and he will be knocked into the water. The owner of the side-show seems to be rehearsing its effectiveness and the black man sits apathetic, hopeless, waiting to be ducked, while the white man bowls heavy wooden balls at him. And suddenly the clown has changed places with him on the ducking-stool.

This episode is vivid. The Negro is transformed. There is laughter and life instead of apathy, and he stands by with the towel that had been round his own neck, ready to dry the clown after his inevitable ducking. More significantly the white man – or is it men? I seem to remember two – become aggressive at a pitch far beyond the depersonalized 'hit the Negro' attitude of our first sight of them. There is violence as he – or they – try to hit the clown, and one of them is reduced to grovelling in the mud on all-fours so as to dirty his hands and get a better grip on the ball. When the clown is ducked the Negro ministers to him, drying him with his towel, and they go off together leaving the ducking-stool empty and the side-show useless.

The next shot is of an Indian magician about to do the trick of stabbing a woman in a box. Again the trick is spoilt by the clown. After the sword-play preliminaries, the magician opens the box to show the admiring crowd that the woman is really there, before performing the stabbing act. The woman is not there. The clown looks out of the box instead with an enormous smile, and the terror of the trick is turned into laughter. As the clown goes on his way we realize that he is being followed by the elephant keeper, the Negro, and now by the Indian magician's woman, as clearly freed from subjection as the Negro is freed from humiliation.

At some time during the film, and I think it is at this point, we are shown the advertisement of a human puppet-show. Magnus, the puppeteer, in a military style uniform is in his private caravan-dressing-room looking into his mirror and preparing for the great act. Beside it is a communal dressing-room-caravan of those who are his puppets, getting ready to be a human Punch and Judy show. They are putting on their make-up and seem to be isolated antagonists. The woman who is 'Judy' is shown snatching a mirror from another member of the cast as she tries to do her hair, and, instead of appearing to be members of an act, each one gives the impression of sullen withdrawal, non-communication.

Magnus the puppeteer and these 'puppets' are shown next in the big top. Punch and Judy and the Hangman are strung up in harnesses to the tent roof. Magnus pulls the strings attached to their limbs as they act out the age-old drama of matrimonial violence with a wooden doll thrown about between them as the baby. Their audience is a crowd of puzzled children, sitting in tiered ranks and dressed in bright-coloured anoraks. There is no laughter in the tent, only camera shots of the half-frightened, half-frightened, half-fascinated children's faces. Then the clown comes in followed by those he has liberated. The camera then shows a pantomime of deliberately distracting the children's attention. While Punch and Judy fight, and the doll puppet is dropped from the ceiling to the floor of the tent, the clown plays a game of cleaning the children's shoes with a feather duster, imitated by his followers, and the children look down at their feet and laugh. Then, leaving the children to his followers, the clown unties the rope that has held the puppets to the tent roof and lowers them. As they step out of their harness he steps into it, just as the group of the furious owners of spoilt side-shows rush into the tent. Magnus angrily yanks the clown upwards in the assumed harness. But first the enemies attack him violently using their side-show weapons. He is badly wounded by the time he is finally lifted beyond their reach. Meanwhile his friends, joined now by the liberated human puppets, clear the tent of the children to save them from the sight of this revenge. As she goes with the rest 'Judy' picks up a living child in her arms.

The tent is left to Magnus, with the clown strung up to the tent roof, powerless and dying. Then the silence of the mime is shattered by his terrible death-cry. The cameras sweep the overcast sky and the empty countryside beyond the circus ground which seems to be filled by its anguish. Then they turn in again to the tent roof and focus first on the dead clown who hangs limp, and then on the booted, uniformed, enthroned Magnus. And Magnus seems to go mad, lashing and jerking the dead clown's limbs with the puppet strings to which they are tied. It is an obscene, cruel, dance of death, with a power-man holding the strings and savagely punishing a strange clown-figure who has put himself into his hands in exchange for his puppets, and who has received into himself the hatred of the tricksters and enslavers. The sequence ends with Magnus alone, exhausted by his anger, the dead clown hanging harnessed above him.

Then it is morning and the cameras show three empty harnesses in the roof of the empty tent.

Meanwhile by the lakeside in the early autumn sunshine there is the group of those whom the clown has liberated. They are bound to each other in their freedom and reverse the picture of alienation which belonged to the human puppet caravan of the day before. Here one holds the mirror for another to shave; the Judy of yesterday and the sari-dressed Indian of the sword act, share a comb.

In his dressing-room-caravan Magnus also looks into his mirror and seems to see his own face for the first time. As he looks, his hand reaches for a jar, and he begins to cover his face with the white of the clown's make-up.

And then the waggons move on, just as at the opening of the film, with a white clown on a white donkey following in their train. He rides tentatively, as one who is at the beginning of a journey.

It is a remarkable film. In the days when I felt I had no language to say the things I wanted to say, it said them to me and for me. Children and young adults who saw it read more into it than I did. When we talked after a showing I was always the learner. I cannot now remember the number of times I have seen it, but those who saw it with me were never satisfied with less than many showings.

Except for one occasion: in the early 1970s I showed it to a group of priests who were making a retreat. They sat silently through its twenty-minute run, and refused a second session. The only comment made at the end was that is seemed to be 'ambivalent about the resurrection'.

That was more than ten years ago, but I am aware that we all too often still look over our shoulders for the answers and certainties of 'Church' when we should be playing our part in the Circus – the Ecclesia of the pilgrim people of God.

Let us then go out to Him, away from the camp, bearing the ignominy he bore; our goal is the city that is one day to be. It is through Him then, that we must offer to God a continual sacrifice of praise, the tribute of lips that give thanks to His name.[2]

2   Hebrews 13:135 (trans. R. A. Knox).